SENECA

TROJAN WOMEN

MASTERS OF LATIN LITERATURE

EDITORS: FREDERICK AHL, DISKIN CLAY,
DOUGLASS PARKER, JON STALLWORTHY

This series aims to help reestablish the importance and intrinsic interest of Latin literature in an age which has rejected the Latin literary model in favor of the Greek. We plan to make available, in modern English-language versions, influential Latin works, especially poetry, from the third century B.C. to the eighteenth century of our own era. By "influential works" we mean not only those commonly read in the classroom today, either in the original or in translation, but also those which shaped literature in their own and in subsequent times, yet have now either lost or been dismissed from their places among the "Great Books" of our culture.

SENECA

TROJAN WOMEN

TRANSLATED AND WITH

AN INTRODUCTION BY

FREDERICK AHL

Cornell University Press

ITHACA AND LONDON

First published 1986 by Cornell University Press
Second printing, with corrections, Cornell Paperbacks, 1996

Printed in the United States of America

Library of Congress Cataloging-in-Publication Data

Seneca, Lucius Annaeus, ca. 4 B.C.–65 A.D.
    Trojan women.

    (Masters of Latin literature)
    Translation of: Troades.
    1. Trojan War—Drama.   2. Troy (Ancient city)—Drama. I.   Ahl, Frederick M.   II. Title.   III. Series.
PA6666.T7A45   1986   872'.01   86-47636
ISBN 0-8014-9431-1 (pbk. : alk. paper)

Cornell University Press strives to use environmentally responsible suppliers and materials to the fullest extent possible in the publishing of its books. Such materials include vegetable-based, low-VOC inks and acid-free papers that are recycled, totally chlorine-free, or partly composed of nonwood fibers. Books that bear the logo of the FSC (Forest Stewardship Council) use paper taken from forests that have been inspected and certified as meeting the highest standards for environmental and social responsibility.
For further information, visit our website
at www.cornellpress.cornell.edu.

5   7   9   Paperback printing   10   8   6

To the memory of Kathleen Mary Cain Ahl

Ní chuala mé in aird sa bhith
ceol ba binne ná do cheol
agus tú fá bhun do nid

Contents

General Introduction

Seneca's Life

Lucius Annaeus Seneca was born in Córdoba, Spain, shortly before the traditional date for the birth of Christ, around 1 B.C., to a family famous and influential in both politics and literature. He was the son of another Lucius Annaeus Seneca (the "Elder"), some of whose works, the *Controversiae* or *Exercises in Persuasion*, survive. His brother, Annaeus Mela, was father of the poet Lucan (Marcus Annaeus Lucanus), author of the *Pharsalia*, an epic poem which tells of the civil wars between Julius Caesar and his military and ideological opponents. Another brother, Lucius Iunius Novatus Gallio (so named because he was adopted by Iunius Gallio), is mentioned in Acts 18:12–18 as the proconsular governor of Achaea in Greece who refused to hear the Jews' case against Paul.

Early Christian writers were aware that the founders of Christianity and the famous philosophical and political family of Seneca were contemporaries. Tertullian describes Seneca as "often one of us,"[1] and there even survives a forged correspondence between Seneca and Paul, full of mutual praise in rather awkward Latin.[2] People found it hard to believe that the world of the Annaei and that of the Christian missionary, which touched in so many ways, should not have pro-

---

[1] *On the Soul* 20.
[2] C. W. Barlow, ed., *Epistolae Senecae ad Paulum et Pauli ad Senecam (Quae Vocantur)* (New York, 1938). Despite the forbidding title, the text is both in Latin and in English translation.

9

duced literary contact, especially since Paul and Seneca both fell victim to the emperor Nero. Paul and, traditionally, other disciples were put to death by Nero during his purge of the Christians in the aftermath of the great fire at Rome (A.D. 64). Similarly, Seneca and members of his family— Gallio, Mela, and Lucan—were all suspected of involvement in a plot to kill Nero the year after the fire (A.D. 65) and obliged to commit suicide.

Although Seneca, like many intellectuals of the first and second centuries A.D. (including his severest ancient critic, the rhetorician Quintilian), was of Spanish origin, he spent most of his life at Rome under the Julio-Claudian imperial dynasty. He was born in Augustus' reign, held his first major political office under Tiberius (A.D. 33), and was a famous orator by the time Caligula succeeded to the throne (A.D. 37). Although his success apparently excited Caligula's jealousy, it was not until the first year of Claudius' reign (A.D. 41) that Seneca first experienced the force of imperial displeasure. He incurred the wrath of Claudius' wife, Messalina, who procured his banishment to the island of Corsica. His recall did not come until A.D. 49, when Claudius' ambitious fourth wife, Agrippina, arranged for him to be tutor to her son, Nero, who became emperor in A.D. 54.

With Seneca's recall in A.D. 49 began the period of his greatest political influence, an ascendancy which lasted until at least A.D. 59, and, in a more limited way, until A.D. 62. Thereafter, Nero appears to have become increasingly suspicious of him. Distrust came to a head with the disclosure of the plot against Nero (A.D. 65), in which Seneca's nephew Lucan apparently played a major role. With the detection of the plot came the downfall not only of Lucan and Seneca, but of most of Seneca's circle of family and friends.

Seneca's Works

Most surviving Roman writers can be handily categorized either as poets or as authors of prose works. Seneca is unusual in that both poetic and prose works attributed to him have survived from antiquity. The poetic works that have come down to us under his name are one historical drama, nine tragedies, which we will discuss shortly, and some epigrams in the *Latin Anthology*. In prose he wrote twelve books of *Dialogues*, the lengthy essays *On Clemency* and *On Benefits*, 124 letters to his friend Lucilius, seven books of *Natural Questions*, and a satire on the death of Claudius, the *Apocolocyntosis*— "*Pumpkinification.*" In these works, Seneca portrays himself as a member of the Stoic school of philosophy, though he frequently cites with admiration—and uses—ideas from rival intellectual groups, notably the Epicureans. Seneca's openness to ideas from different philosophical schools makes an interesting contrast with the hostility other philosophical writers of the first and second centuries A.D. show towards their intellectual opponents. To give two illustrative examples: The closest surviving ancient parallels to Seneca's satirical *Apocolocyntosis* are probably the *Dialogues of the Gods*, written by the Greek Epicurean Lucian a century or so later. Lucian is not nearly so kind to the Stoics, however, as Seneca is to the Epicureans. He mocks them mercilessly. Similarly, the closest parallel to Seneca's famous treatise *On Anger*, included among the *Dialogues*, is Plutarch's *On Anger*. Plutarch, however, had no patience with Stoicism and wrote two stinging essays, along with extensive negative comments elsewhere, attacking what he considered the absurdities of Stoic philosophy: *On Stoic Self-Contradictions* and *Against the Stoics on Common Conceptions*.

I mention these points because scholars sometimes interpret Seneca's poetry not just in terms of the Stoic elements in his philosophical prose, but as if he were an embodiment of the fundamentalist puritanism we find in Lucian's Stoic caricatures. They thus discover in his tragedies a kind of drama of Stoic dogmatism which accords ill with Seneca's—and Stoic—eclecticism, and with the Stoics' preoccupation with paradox. Yet even if we choose to believe Seneca was a Stoic zealot of the sort Lucian mocks, we do not have to see him as a soul that is self-confident and at spiritual peace. The religious and philosophical agonies of Milton or, no less poignantly, Donne, should warn us of the terrible "laceration of mind," as Samuel Johnson calls it, with which deep-seated religious feelings and conversions are associated. The same John Donne can, in other moods and times, produce the erotic flippancy of *The Flea* and the melancholy religious brilliance of *A Hymne to God the Father*. Similarly, Seneca will sometimes assure us of the invincibility of good, at other times confront us with the apparently inevitable triumph of evil.

The believer may struggle for footing over an abyss of atheism that the conventionally pious or the mere agnostic cannot begin to comprehend. Indeed, the eclecticism of Seneca's prose works might even emanate from the tolerance born in one who has experienced the agony of the abyss. Plato's Socrates in *Republic* 8–10 recognizes and fears the force of evil within the soul, the beast that awakens when the rational part of the mind is asleep. This irrational element, the mythical beast, must, he felt, be suppressed in each of us just as poetry must be suppressed within the state, at least in part because it gives form to the nightmarish and irrational. But to argue for the suppression of a passion or of an artistic form is to acknowledge one's fear of its power.

Seneca, unlike Plato, gives us two separate visions: the rational, philosophical obverse of his paradoxical coin and the poetical reverse. In fact, it is hard to be sure which side is the front and which the back of the Senecan coin. To get the complete picture, we must of course consider both. Nonetheless, it is entirely possible to contemplate each face separately. Students of Senecan philosophy have had no qualms about omitting discussion of the tragedies. Poets, therefore, have a precedent for the same sort of omission, but in reverse. We will, I would argue, gain a better picture of Seneca's poetry— and perhaps of his prose too—if we consider his tragedies, at least at first, *apart from* his prose works. For to do so will help us counteract a widely held but usually false assumption that poetry begins its existence as prose, and is, essentially, no more than a kind of ornate prose.

The manuscript tradition of Seneca's tragedies aids our task. For the plays, in fact, survived from antiquity separately from the prose works. Centuries ago it was thought that the poetry and prose were the works of two distinct persons: a tragic Seneca and a philosophical Seneca. So the question naturally arises: How do we know that the tragedies and the prose works were written by the same hand? Quintilian's quotation of *Medea* 354 in *Instructing the Orator* 9.2.8 is the only evidence that someone named Seneca actually wrote any of the plays that have come down to us under this name. Quintilian's phrase, "like Medea in Seneca," shows that (a) Seneca wrote it. But Quintilian may mean the Elder Seneca, as he clearly does later in the same chapter (9.2.42).

Settling the Senecan authorship of *Medea* still leaves unresolved the question as to whether the other nine plays included in the Senecan corpus are also by a Seneca. There is general consensus that one, *Octavia*, is not his work, and serious doubts have been raised about another, *Hercules on Oeta*. Most scholars accept the authenticity of the remaining seven—*Hercules in His Madness*, *Trojan Women*, *Phoenician Women*, *Phaedra*, *Oedipus*, *Agamemnon*, and *Thyestes*—even though, as we have seen, none of them is attested as Senecan by an ancient writer. I accept the judgment of scholars on the matter of the plays' authenticity, though I have a nagging suspicion that the *Elder* Seneca wrote *Phaedra* and, possibly, other plays.

Dating the Plays

Seneca is one of only a handful of Romans of senatorial rank before the fourth century A.D. who have survived to us as poets in their own right. Curiously, his most notable fellow aristocratic poets are his near contemporaries: his short-lived nephew Lucan (A.D. 39–65), author of the *Pharsalia*, and Silius Italicus (A.D. 25–101), author of the *Punica*. Like Lucan, and unlike Silius, Seneca appears to have written poetry while he was politically active. Yet Seneca differs sharply from Lucan as well as from Silius in several major respects. To begin with, they wrote epic, the most "elevated" of Roman poetic forms, and their epics show the self-confident moral and historical judgment that characterizes Roman senatorial writing. Their style is evocative of the aristocratic historians Sallust and Tacitus. They write of Rome itself, they lament the passage of a pluralistic, republican state. One is always aware of their Romanness and of the age in which they are writing.

Seneca, in contrast, not only chose tragedy, a literary form that had, by his time, ceased to be a major vehicle of poetic or political statement, but seems calculatedly to have avoided specific references both to his own day and to things Roman. Among the ten plays attributed to him, only *Octavia* deals with a contemporary subject. And few scholars now claim that this play was actually written by Seneca. In fact, Seneca is a character in it.

With the exception, then, of the *Octavia*, the plays attributed to Seneca present so few overt and recognizably Roman elements that

13

we are startled when we come upon them. This lack of contemporary reference makes dating the plays virtually impossible. The prose works, in contrast, are of much more certain date, ranging from his *Consolation to Marcia* (included among the *Dialogues*) in A.D. 41 to his *Natural Questions* and *Letters to Lucilius*, both published between A.D. 63 and 65.

Although the traditional, mythical topics Seneca selects for his plays are as obviously appropriate to the world of the early emperors at Rome as the mythical epics written by Statius and Valerius Flaccus in the decades just after Seneca's death, Seneca affords us no clues, as Statius does, about when his work was written and about what contemporary experience it refracts. We can hardly move beyond generalization. True, Seneca's plays, with the possible exception of *Phaedra*, mirror a top-heavy Roman world of absolute power as surely as Athenian tragedy mirrors the often chaotic Greek democracy and intellectual pluralism of Athens in the fifth century B.C. But, as Seneca lived his whole life under the imperial autocracy, we have not said much when we have said that.

Since dating the plays on external evidence and internal contemporary commentary is impossible, the best we can do is establish some probable sequence of their composition on the basis of internal stylistic considerations, as John Fitch has done.[3] Fitch accepts the general dating of *Hercules in His Madness* to before 54 B.C. This was the year of Claudius' death and Nero's accession to the throne. And one of Seneca's own works, the *Apocolocyntosis,* "*Pumpkinification,*" parodies a lament from *Hercules in His Madness*. Fitch's study suggests that *Trojan Women* and *Medea* belong to approximately the same time period and that *Phaedra*, *Oedipus*, and *Agamemnon* are earlier. How much earlier, however, we cannot say. The fragmentary *Phoenician Women* and *Thyestes* were, according to Fitch's analysis written later, during the last decade of Seneca's life.

If Fitch is right—and there is no certain means of telling whether he is or not—Seneca's plays were written at various points throughout his life, but most *before* Nero's reign.

---

[3] "Sense-Pauses and Relative Dating in Seneca, Sophocles, and Shakespeare," *American Journal of Philology* 102 (1981): 289–307.

Critics and Admirers

Seneca was one of the most influential political, intellectual, and literary figures whose works survive to us from antiquity. He shaped the development of the tragic drama in Renaissance Europe, he inspired and influenced literary and intellectual figures as different as Montaigne and Calvin. In short, his appeal to creative writers has been immense. Yet the reader of modern articles and books about Seneca is more likely to encounter unfavorable than favorable critical evaluations of his work.

Hostility to Seneca is hardly new. From his own day on, Seneca's work and character have endured severe attacks from what we might loosely term the academic establishment. Writing less than a generation after Seneca's death, the rhetorician Quintilian takes him to task for a variety of errors in judgment and in style: the researchers he employed made mistakes; Seneca himself used "unnatural" expressions and strove to achieve a kind of terse "quotability." Seneca was, it seemed, a dangerous and potentially corrupting influence on a schoolboy's style of writing. Quintilian's reaction to Seneca was so strongly negative that some of his contemporaries thought it arose from personal loathing—an allegation Quintilian feels constrained to deny in his *Instructing the Orator*. The Roman historian Tacitus, writing shortly after Quintilian, passes similarly scathing judgment on Seneca's character: he was a hypocritically pious moralist with bloodied hands who lacked the courage of his convictions.

The negative scholarly view of Seneca did not gain the upper hand until the last two centuries, however. For the preceding millennium and a half, Seneca retained his following outside the classroom. Indeed, it was his enormous popularity as a literary figure in Quintilian's day which prompted the scholar to treat him at length, and in a special category apart from other writers, as a subversive literary model. After the early nineteenth century, however, Seneca lost his wide and admiring audience. Quintilian's anxieties about Seneca's corrupting influence were echoed by many Latin teachers who chose to instruct their students in the prose style of Caesar and Cicero and in the verse of Horace and Vergil. These teachers, too, found Seneca a corrupting influence who did not fit, and therefore undermined, firmly held notions of what a classical author should be both stylistically and morally. Seneca, like Apuleius and Statius, had to be rejected, however important he may have been in shaping Western literature, because he was "late," decadent, and "not classical." He did not represent the kind of Latinity, the period of Roman history, or the perspective on the Roman world that academics wanted to teach. And Seneca's critics found in Quintilian and Tacitus stylistic and moral justification for rejecting him.

Nineteenth- and twentieth-century scholarly antagonism to Seneca proved more damaging than Quintilian's attacks precisely because Seneca had lost his wider audience outside academia. It is important to understand, however, that his diminished popularity was not testimony to a change in literary tastes, as is sometimes suggested, but to the fact that Latin literature as a whole had become increasingly the exclusive and dwindling domain of academics who often seemed curiously determined to show how distasteful most of it was while lamenting that people were neglecting it. No field of literary study rivals that of Latin poetry in so systematically belittling the quality of its works and authors. And no field of literary study more thoroughly quarantines itself from contemporary critical thought. As a result, in many colleges Seneca is outside the still decreasing canon of academically "approved" writers, as are the overwhelming majority of ancient writers whose works are extant but unread even in excerpts.

Latinists often forget how many of the "faults" for which they denounce Seneca and other Roman writers are, in fact, the usual goals towards which poets and essayists strive: to make the language their own rather than to follow scholastically prescribed usage; to avail themselves of all the resonances of meaning their language can bear; to achieve the memorable, the quotable. The criticisms directed against Seneca by Quintilian and his successors could even more justifiably be leveled against Shakespeare: he, too, made mistakes in research, used "unnatural" expressions, and strove to achieve terse "quotability."

But recently the picture has been changing. Major critical editions of Senecan tragedy by Tarrant (*Agamemnon, Thyestes*), Fantham (*Tro-*

jan Women), Fitch's *Hercules* and Costa's smaller *Medea* have begun to focus classicists' attention on Senecan drama. And although—or rather because—Seneca has ceased to be canonical reading, interest in his works, especially in his tragedies, has gradually reawakened among poets, historians of the theater, and Shakespearean critics. The ascendancy of what scholars and directors alike have taken to be the Greek model of tragedy became so marked and ubiquitous by the middle of the twentieth century that the Greek muse was no longer exotic. Sophocles seemed familiar. The Roman Seneca now became the remote, primitive, and mysterious writer. Roman tragedy had been absent from the canonical reading of our culture long enough for its rediscovery to be exciting and artistically stimulating. It was "other," it was malleable, it was the stuff of experiment and innovation in the theater. And that, Ted Hughes observed, is why Peter Brook wanted to produce Seneca's, not Sophocles', *Oedipus* in London at the Old Vic in 1968.

The differences between Senecan and Athenian tragedy are often—as they were to the producers of Ted Hughes' adaptation of Seneca's *Oedipus*—precisely the strength and theatrical allure of the Latin dramas. As Hughes wrote in his introduction to *Oedipus*, "the Greek world saturates Sophocles too thoroughly: the evolution of his play seems complete, fully explored and in spite of its blood-roots, fully civilized. The figures in Seneca's *Oedipus* are Greek only by convention: by nature they are more primitive than aboriginals . . . . Seneca hardly notices the intricate moral possibilities of his subject."[4]

I do not much agree with Hughes' assessment of Senecan as opposed to Sophoclean drama, since I believe that Sophocles, no less than Seneca, has been distorted by the puzzling modern desire to treat tragedies as moral and religious sermons. But this disagreement is beside the point. Hughes' essential point is, I think, correct: Senecan tragedy is vastly and intriguingly different from Greek tragedy. To contend that Seneca is doing no more than rendering some extant or nonextant Greek original is to do him the injustice that scholars have finally, I hope, stopped doing Plautus. The contrast, then, between Hughes' notion of Senecan tragedy and the conventional scholarly

[4] *Seneca's "Oedipus,"* adapted by Ted Hughes (London, 1969), p. 8.

view of Seneca could hardly be more total. Hughes is delighted that Seneca is un-Greek; classicists are upset that Seneca is not Greek enough.

Seneca's characters are more introspective and self-analyzing than even a Sophoclean Ajax. Their most critical battles, like the critical battles of many a Shakespearean character, are often those that they fight with themselves. Senecan drama constantly takes us beyond a character's words into his or her very thoughts, keeping us aware of the tension between what someone says and does and what that same person perceives as the reason for what is said and done. We see a character's hopes, illusions, and delusions played out before us.

Seneca and the Theater

Increased theatrical interest in Senecan tragedy contrasts with scholastic insistence that Senecan tragedy was never actually staged at Rome. We will never know if and how Senecan tragedy was staged. It is probably correct that Seneca's *Oedipus* was not produced before the massed citizen body of Rome as Sophocles' *Oedipus* was produced before the citizen body of Athens. But this does not mean it was not designed for performance and actually performed in small gatherings, as we shall see. Much modern drama is not aimed at, or performed before, a broad national audience either. Despite the accessibility of mass audiences through television and cinema, the contemporary writer often chooses to address a literary elite in a small theater.

Although Seneca clearly writes for an elite too, his plays deal with and direct themselves towards the powerful, as most modern theater in the English language does not. Senecan tragedy, like Greek, is about power and about those who exercise it, and it addresses the issues of power through the language of myth. It does not name contemporary names; it speaks through traditional characters drawn ultimately from an ancient poetic tradition whose roots extend back into the second millennium B.C. and beyond. Yet the fact that Senecan tragedy deals with and directs itself to the powerful is the reason it can be seen not only to resemble classical Greek tragedy but, paradoxically, to differ from Greek tragedy when one inspects it more closely.

During the Athenian democracy, poetic expression was dominantly theatrical. The Athenian audience that listened in the theater voted in the assembly; poets, like the popular leaders, sought to reach it and persuade it. Roman poets of the early empire, and those of pre- and post- democratic Greece, directed their work to the literate ruling classes, and shied away from "popular" drama. First, the populace had no political power in imperial Rome. It could not even vote to elect magistrates. That is why I find the Chorus' remarks in *Phaedra* 982–984 perplexing. Its words seem to suggest that the populace exercises a political role which it did not in Seneca's day:

> fraud rules as despot   in the halls of power,
> the people find joy   in giving high office [*fasces*]
> to a vile man. They   adore those they hate most.

Second, under the Roman emperors it was difficult and dangerous, as well as, apparently, futile, to communicate with the popular audience. If a popular audience detected a covert insult or jest at the emperor's expense, it might be unsophisticated enough to roar its recognition, approving or disapproving, aloud—to the great peril of the writer. Smaller, more refined audiences, meeting in times of tyranny and in gatherings where names are known, react more cautiously. Experience teaches them that to acknowledge the insult or the jest, or even to be present when it is made, imperils the listener as well as the author. That is why, in a notorious incident mentioned by the biographer Suetonius in his life of Seneca's nephew Lucan, the people in a public restroom fled when Lucan, while breaking wind noisily, quoted a half-line written by the emperor Nero.

Besides, the literary theater never enjoyed in Rome the official state support it had in Athens. There were no permanent theaters until Pompey built one in 55 B.C. And that great general built it to give himself, not dramatists, a stage. Actors, as well as some playwrights, were often slaves or former slaves, not members of a fashionable profession. Further, dramatists had to compete for the public's attention with spectacles of increasing scale and extravagance that were underwritten by the wealthy and sanctioned by ritual practice. The Latin word *munus*, suggesting a public offering or service, came to be shorthand for a gladiatorial "offering." Such ritual and circus-like entertainments were features of Roman life from the middle of the third century B.C. on. The ruling classes stressed the spectacular and underplayed the verbal and intellectual dimensions so fundamental to Greek drama. Terence, the comic playwright, in the prologue to *The Mother- in-Law*, says it was impossible to hold one's own against the competition of a tightrope walker. Holding one's own against a gladiatorial "offering" would have been no easier.

The poet Horace, writing in Rome a generation or two before Seneca, tells Octavian, the imperial Augustus, that Democritus—"the laughing philosopher," as he was called—would guffaw at the notion that a dramatist could win the attention of his restive audience: "he would think the writers were creating their play for an ass—and a deaf one. What voices have had power enough to overwhelm the noise which echoes round our theaters?" (Horace *Epistles* 2.1.199–201). Pleasure, Horace adds, has "shifted from the ear to eyes that are not good at seeing" (*Epistles* 2.1.187–188), even among the Equestrian order, the Roman upper middle class. And, he continues in the lines immediately following, not only games but triumphal processions celebrating military victories have intruded upon the dramatist's stage.

Horace' last comment has a special pungency in this epistle, addressed as it is to Octavian, who had been the victor in a savage civil war and was the conqueror and imperial ruler of Rome. If the biographer Suetonius is right in his claim that this poem is Horace's response to Octavian's complaint of exclusion from Horace's *sermones*, his "conversations"—the works we know as his *Satires* and *Epistles*—Horace is suggesting that the emperor, as principal giver of games and sole giver of triumphs, has usurped the dramatist's place in the theater. The theater is owned by the emperor and stages only his shows. Hence Horace's expressed desire to entrust himself to a *reader* rather than to a spectator (*Epistles* 2.1.214–218). The language and metaphor he uses are more appropriate to the arena and the hippodrome than to the muses and god of poetry. They suggest that Octavian thinks more in terms of a *munus*, "offering," than of poetry itself. He wants books that will fight for him like gladiators, that will serve his glory. The theater already exists for the emperor's glory; the threat lurks that all literature will come to serve the same purpose.

For Octavian now wishes to intrude himself into the poet's private "conversations."

Octavian was, in fact, more eager to censor published and *durable* poetry than the more fleeting criticism which might occur in a public performance. Ovid, who died in exile when Seneca was in his teens, chastises Octavian for being so concerned about morality in poetry but so unconcerned about the blatant immorality of what is represented in the theater and at the emperor's own games, before his very eyes (*Tristia* 2.497–546). In *Tristia* 5.7.25–30, Ovid comments on the irony of his own situation in this regard: some of his poetry has been adapted for and performed in the theater, although he himself claims: "I have—and you know this yourself—written nothing for the theater." Incidentally, if we take Ovid at his work here, the two lines said to have survived from his play *Medea* would seem either not to be genuinely his or to be adapted from his treatments of Medea elsewhere in his poetry. He may, of course, have written the work for reading or performance elsewhere than in the public theater. Still, in his exile, he says, he takes some consolation in the thought that his poems, adapted for the theater, keep his memory and name alive in Rome.

The theater, then, was seen by both poet and political leader in the generations preceding Seneca not only as a noisy place, unconducive to poetry, but as a vehicle of corruption and political propaganda. Succeeding Roman emperors, particularly Nero and Domitian, were also well aware of the theater's power. Domitian banned actors from the public stage. Nero adopted a much different approach. Part of his own immense popularity—and much of the contempt that men of letters felt for him—stemmed from his appearances as a performer in the theater and the hippodrome.

Despite their reluctance to write for the popular stage, Roman writers were aware—in Ovid's case poignantly aware—that performances in the theater have a power over the popular imagination that "pure" poetry lacks, and they regularly presented human activity in terms of the theater or amphitheater. In his *Aeneid*, Vergil describes the landscape of North Africa as a *scaena*, a stage set, and compares the nightmarish visions of Queen Dido to the horror experienced on stage by Pentheus or Orestes. When Aeneas visits the new Troy built by Andromache, he walks in on a tragic tableau: a mock Troy frozen in time, as if in a painting or stage set, with Andromache lamenting, as ever, over an empty grave honoring her dead husband, Hector. The characters of Latin poetry also see themselves theatrically or amphitheatrically. In Lucan's *Pharsalia*, Pompey, builder of Rome's first permanent theater, dreams of his past triumphs in theatrical imagery. As he dies, he behaves like an actor who must win approval for his final scene. Lucan, in fact, gives an important role in the *Pharsalia* to the man who invented the amphitheater: Scribonius Curio. And this Curio, we are told by the historian and naturalist Pliny, a contemporary of Seneca's, was the same man who maneuvered the opposing political factions of the Roman state into civil war, much as he turned his two back-to-back theaters into one amphitheater to stage a grand gladiatorial contest.

Seneca presents life in terms of the arena both in his tragedies and in his philosophical works. In his essay *On Providence* he dismisses ordinary gladiatorial shows as "the childish delights of human vanity" and asks us to contemplate instead the greatest contest of them all: "a matched pair worthy of god's eyes—a brave man pitted against an evil destiny, with the brave man as challenger." In his tragedies, particularly *Trojan Women*, many motifs suggest a theater far different from that of Aeschylus or Euripides. The site of Polyxena's sacrifice on Achilles' tomb, for example, is described as if it were part of a *munus*, an offering, in the amphitheater (*Trojan Women* 1123–1126):

> on the other side,
> it [the tomb] is encompassed by a plain, rising
> gently at the edges to create
> a valley in between—the shape suggests
> a theater, in fact.

Astyanax' death has much the same "theatrical" quality. The dramatist asks his audience and readers to envisage the scene from Greek myth in terms of the familiar horror of ritual death in the Roman theater. And he asks them to censure those who hated what they saw but watched anyway. Roman readers could hardly fail to see themselves reflected in the Senecan mirror, much as they would see themselves in the equally stinging comment in the passage from *Phaedra*, cited earlier, that they worship those holders of the *fasces* (the Roman symbols of public office) whom they hate. Yet Seneca is aware that he, like his morally critical messenger, is himself as guilty of hypocrisy as those he criticizes.

At least one of Seneca's tragic characters, the messenger whom I would identify with Talthybius in *Trojan Women*, recognizes how sacrificial and gladiatorial death affects the spectator: desire to watch vying with hatred of what one watches. Seneca understands that part of his audience will see the victims as heroic and that such heroism is beyond words. The doomed Polyxena in *Trojan Women* does not speak; Astyanax says only "Pity me, mother." In the verbal environment of tragedy, the sacrificial heroes themselves do not speak. They, like the Chorus envisaging cosmic catastrophe in the *Thyestes*, invite the listener or reader to imagine, not to hear. Seneca, like other great writers of Roman imperial times, often creates images for the mind's eye rather than for strictly visual perception.

The model that Seneca's Roman reader or listener used as his imagination wandered could be drawn from memories of the countless silent "performers" who died each year at Roman games. This same amphitheatrical notion of heroic death helped the growth of Christianity. The martyrs who died in the arena recalled the secularized contests to their ritual origins. And the horror of their suffering fixed another myth in men's minds.

To interest a popular Roman audience in a stage "death" when the games afforded ample opportunity to see real death must have been difficult. The dramatist could not compete, and probably would not have wanted to compete, with the grim spectacles Martial, a poet of the generation after Seneca, describes in his *Book of Spectacles*. The Roman amphitheater imparted to even the grossest and most grisly myths a certain air of reality. The emperor Titus staged not only Hercules' labors at the games in real-life performances but the consummation of the Cretan queen Pasiphae's obsessive passion for a bull. Pasiphae was the wife of Minos, king of Crete, and she was helped in her desire to mate with the bull by the Athenian artist Daedalus, who designed a cowsuit for her to wear so that the bull would mistake her for a heifer. Her child by this union was, of course, the famous Minotaur:

Believe it now! Pasiphae did make it with the Cretan bull;
  We've seen it happen; the old story now has credibility.
Yet ancient folklore should not take the credit for itself:
  Caesar, your circus actors make *all* folksongs live for you.

In the following poems Martial reiterates his point about the "realization" of myth on stage. Poem 7 is the culmination of the series.:

Just as Prometheus, bound tight on a Russian crag
Fed with his ever-healing and regrowing heart
The bird that never tires of eating
                    So,
                        cast as Laureolus,
The bandit-king, nailed to a cross (no stage-prop this)
The unknown actor showed his raw guts to a Highland bear.
His shredded limbs clung onto life although
Their bits and pieces gushed with blood:
No trace of body—but the body lived.
Finally he got the punishment he deserved . . . [5]
  Maybe he'd slit his master's throat, the thug;
  Maybe he'd robbed a temple treasury of gold, mad fool;
  Maybe he'd tried to burn our city, Rome.
The criminal responsible surpassed all ancient folklore's crimes.
Through him what had been merely myth became
  Real punishment.

The condemned criminal—whose crime, we note, no one seems to know for sure—is condemned to act out the role of Laureolus, the bandit-king, crucified in the arena.

The cruelty Martial describes was not Titus' invention. Titus was merely continuing a tradition begun by the emperor Caligula. Suetonius, the biographer of the earliest emperors, describes the bloody competition for the role of Laureolus in Caligula's day in his *Life of Caligula*. But what Martial sets first in our minds is the myth of Prometheus: the benefactor of mankind, enduring the daily attacks of the bird that fed on his liver and knowing the secret that would

---

[5] Part of the line is lost in our texts.

bring about the downfall of his tormentor, the god Jupiter. The comparison with the man playing Laureolus, then, horrifies with its appropriate inappropriateness. Myth tells us how Prometheus offended Jupiter, but it also reassures us of his ultimate release by Hercules. Martial's nameless criminal, however, guilty of crimes unknown, will have no Hercules to free him, and a wild bear, not a surgically precise bird's beak, will torment him. The poor substitute Laureolus, whatever he did, earns the status of Prometheus, which, in this incident, gives him a greater claim to divinity than any of the emperors who often pretended that they were themselves gods: Jupiter incarnate. Martial's Laureolus walks the same "stage" as the suffering Christ.

Martial, the poet-artist, does not specifically thank his emperor for this demonstration of myth's viability (as he thanks him in each of the preceding poems), surely because the poem is a terrible indictment of what his eyes have seen and thus of whoever it was that organized the grim spectacle. Martial had some reason to be cautious. For, as poem 8 makes clear, the artist himself may endure a similarly mythlike fate:

Artistic Daedalus:
When you were being wolfed and mangled by that bear
How you must have wished you now had your wings!

Daedalus, having helped Pasiphae mate with the bull, later designed the labyrinth to conceal her child. He also helped Theseus kill the beast and escape with Minos' daughter Ariadne. Understandably, he lost his royal master's favor. Minos imprisoned him in his own work of art. Daedalus escaped by inventing wings and flying out. Martial's latter-day Daedalus, however, out of favor with his Minos, has no wings to escape his enraged master and the carnivorous beast.

The Roman imperial poet's task was dauntingly Daedalus-like. Aware that he served an often cruel master, he had to communicate without ending up like Martial's Daedalus. The poet knew he could not compete for an audience of the moment with the spectacle, with the reality of Roman theatrical death. He could not even express his full disgust with that spectacle, his horror at it—much less attempt to aid its victims—without risking a terrible fate himself. In the first satire of Juvenal, a near contemporary of Martial, we are told of a critic whose charred corpse inscribes a black line in the sand of the theater after he has been used as a human torch to light the arena. The poet risks being transformed from a writer into a pen with which others write. Hence, perhaps, his flight from and fascination with the theater, his preference for epic and for myth. As Martial shows, only myth could express the extent of the horror of what was happening precisely *because* even myth paled in comparison with the staged reality. Life, as presented in the arena, had become an imitation of art. Ovid, in his *Metamorphoses*, suggests it always had been.

Staging the Plays

Senecan tragedy demands performance, not just recitation by two or three readers. The rapid interchanges between, say Medea (or Phaedra) and her nurse need actors, not just voices. The commonly held view that the plays were recited by a single voice assumes that the Latin terms *recitare* and *recitatio* carry the same sense as the English "recite" and "recitation." There is no reason, however, to suppose that they preclude the notion of performance by multiple actors, as much as *recitare* does in Italian theatrical parlance. *Recitare un dramma* means "to perform a play," not "to recite a play." What is sometimes called the "Recitation theory" of Senecan tragedy owes much to this restrictive Anglo-German-French sense of what *recitatio* must have been.[6]

None of the complete plays attributed to Seneca presents major staging problems to a director, much less difficulties comparable to those found in such Greek tragedies as Sophocles' *Ajax* or Aeschylus' *Eumenides* (which *were* publicly performed). Once we accept Senecan tragedy as designed for performance, we may appreciate better some of the remarkable effects, actual and potential, in the staging of *Phaedra*, *Medea*, and *Trojan Women*. In *Trojan Women*, for instance, Seneca brings Pyrrhus onstage to take Polyxena away to be sacrificed. Pyrrhus and Polyxena move but do not speak. Yet they are spoken

---

[6] *Seneca's "Troades": A Literary Introduction with Text, Translation, and Commentary* (Princeton, 1982), p. 49. See also Dana Sutton's excellent *Seneca on the Stage*, Mnemosyne Supplement 96 (Leiden, 1986).

to by Hecuba and Andromache. In forceful contrast, Hecuba and Andromache, though they speak, are not involved in the *action* of the scene.

Yet if, as I have suggested, the plays were designed for performance but not performed in public theaters, were they only plays in search of a stage, or were they performed but in a less public manner? The germ of an answer is found in Suetonius' *Domitian* 7. Domitian, we are told, "forbade actors to use the [outdoor, public] stage, but conceded to them the right to practice their art indoors." Domitian's action, of course, was taken some thirty years after Seneca's death. But the practice of "in-house" performances may well have been going on for some time before Domitian's decree. And this, I believe, is how Senecan tragedy was performed: in the more than ample homes of well-to-do Romans. I emphasize that my resolution of the problem is no more than a matter of personal opinion—as are other theories about the performance or nonperformance of the plays. I also warn the reader that stage directions given in the translations are only my suggestions. Recall, however, that stage directions found in translations of Greek tragedy are also the work of a translator—though he or she does not always acknowledge this to be the case.

Ultimately the question as to how Senecan tragedy was presented matters more to a historian of the theater than to a director. The real question for the director is whether he would find one of these plays stageworthy if he had a usable script in hand. And here is the major problem: there are few English versions of Senecan tragedy and even fewer which suggest that the plays are stageworthy. My aim has been to produce stageable versions of the plays without resorting to adaptation rather than translation and without sacrificing the poetry in an effort to achieve colloquial realism. For Senecan tragedy, like Shakespearean or Greek tragedy, is a poetic form, not just a dramatic one.

About the Translations

Translating Seneca is hampered not only by critical prejudice against the plays but by an increasing tendency to disparage Latin literature as a whole. Latin has been for centuries the language of learning and of pretentiousness. And, unlike Greek, its latter-day scholastic rival, it has a rather English appearance, since so many English words are derived either directly or indirectly from Latin. It is remote enough to appear abstract and pedantic but too familiar to seem exotic. If Erich Auerbach had called his book *Imitatio* rather than *Mimesis*, it would probably have had less appeal. To caricature the popular stereotypes: the Greeks, who were imaginative, practiced mimesis; the Romans, good at building arches but less adept at poetry and philosophy, practiced imitation. These stereotypes are well established in English-speaking societies. And Latinists themselves are largely responsible for them.

Although many English words look as if they should be equivalents for their Latin ancestors, they often differ greatly in meaning or "feel." We would rarely assume that the character of a remote ancestor can correctly be assessed by analyzing the character of a modern descendant of the same name. Yet we are sometimes less than cautious in making similar assumptions about English words of Latin ancestry. "Accept," for example, derives from the Latin *accipere*, which means something like "to take to oneself." The English "accept" lacks the aggressive sense of *accipere*. It comes from a passive form of the Latin verb and retains a sense of passivity, as do a great many words used in Latinate English. The lethargy of the descendants belies their ancestral vigor. Yet popular dictionaries and translations still use the descendants to represent their forefathers, largely because scholars cannot agree on alternatives. "Virtue," derived from *virtus*, is a good instance, especially because here we are concerned with a Roman writer who had much to say about *virtus*. Ancient Roman *virtus*, not out of place on the battlefield, evolved into the now obsolete "virtue" as philosophers, moralists, and monks adapted it for use in a sexual context.[7] At the beginning of the twentieth century Francis Cornford,

---

[7] "Virtue," in all likelihood, died when its own adjective, "virtuous," was found unacceptable by movie censors in Hollywood in the 1930s. Presumably virtue's foes realized that if someone were described as "not virtuous," audiences would naturally assume that he or she was sexually active. Mention of sexual activity was taboo in English and American films of the period. The RKO studio therefore instructed its writers to avoid words which suggested physical sexuality, however obliquely. "Virtuous" was one of the words proscribed (as was "nursery"). See K. MacGowan, *Behind the Screen* (New York, 1965), p. 358.

in the introduction to his translation of Plato's *Republic*, satirized the use of "virtue" as a translation for the Greek *arete*: "One who opened Jowett's version at random and lighted on the statement . . . that the best guardian for a man's 'virtue' is 'philosophy tempered with music,' might run away with the idea that, in order to avoid irregular relations with women, he had better play the violin in the intervals of studying metaphysics.'"[8] Subsequent Greek scholars have dealt with the problem not by seeking another equivalent but by adopting *arete* into their usage as a translation for itself. Latinists, in contrast, generally retain "virtue" for *virtus*. Those embarrassed by "virtue" yet fearful of scholarly scorn for using an English term which misses many nuances of *virtus* cautiously imitate the Hellenist and use *virtus* as a translation for itself. Such subterfuge is available to the scholarly commentator but not to the translator. And I have tried to avoid it. Obviously my choice, "manliness," will not please everyone. But it does try to bring out the force of *vir*, "man," in *virtus* even though it cannot catch the paradoxically feminine gender of the Latin original.

The translator must take into account other differences between Latin and English. Latin is compact and polysyllabic. English is more monosyllabic and far more compact. There are inevitably more words in an English sentence than in its Latin original, but not necessarily more *syllables*. I have tried to keep the number of syllables in my English approximately equal to the number of syllables in Seneca's Latin. Since the English iambic pentameter used here in place of the Latin trimeter is syllabically shorter, however, there are more lines in my English then in the Latin. For the reader's convenience, I mark the line numbers of the Latin original in the margins.

To convey the force and style of Senecan tragedy, something must be done with his ubiquitous wordplay. It is insufficient, when translating poetry, to select the word in language *A* which most closely approximates what scholars take to be the meaning of a given word in language *B*. Poetic word selection is rarely governed exclusively, or even largely, by considerations of what teachers call "literal" meaning. Seneca, like many poets, ancient and modern, creates a richly allusive text where the "literal" meaning of a word often explodes into wordplay of multiple resonances suggested by the context in

---

[8] *The "Republic" of Plato*, trans. F. M. Cornford (Oxford, 1941), p. vi.

which it is set. I render the wordplays I have detected (puns, anagrams, and so forth) by equivalent plays in English.

My translations aim at a formal but not stuffy American literary and poetic idiom, interspersed, where appropriate, with a more colloquial style to underscore changes of mood and tone in the original. A few residual Anglicisms from my British childhood may have crept in too. At the same time, I have avoided such Americanisms as might appear stridently alien in other English-speaking countries. My usage may therefore seem synthetic and artificially neutral. I would defend my choices in these matters on the grounds that Senecan tragedy is itself formal in style and diction, and in verse. The tragedies are poetry and cannot be transposed satisfactorily into modern, colloquial prose drama without radical departures from the structure of the original.

I found that each Senecan play had a very individual "feel." The characters are quite distinct from one another even when they have similar roles. Thus the nurse in the *Phaedra* and the nurse in the *Medea* are as distinctive as the protagonists they serve. Indeed, no preconception about Senecan drama strikes me as more fundamentally incorrect than the notion that each play is essentially a variant of one plot, rehashed with characters of a dull sameness. As I translated, what surprised me most was the ironic wit of such characters as Pyrrhus and the humorous yet horrifying pomposity of Agamemnon in the *Trojan Women*. It had not occurred to me before that Seneca, like Euripides, might be capable of enhancing our sense of horror by evoking laughter.

My approach to each play is different, partly by design, partly by accident. The elaborate choral metrics of the *Phaedra* seemed to need a more elaborate English response than the delectable but less complex metrics of the *Trojan Women*. So I chose to approximate the Latin meters more closely in the *Phaedra* than in the *Trojan Women*. On the other hand, I prepared these translations over a period of some fifteen years, finishing the *Trojan Women* first and the *Phaedra* last. During that period my approach to Latin poetry and translation has changed considerably. But I have tried not to edit out my earlier perceptions of the *Trojan Women*, my personal favorite among the tragedies. I believe it to be the finest piece of theater Seneca produced, comparable with the best of Greek drama.

Questions the Plays May Prompt

Seneca clearly assumed that his audience or readers were intimately familiar with Greco-Roman myth. To help the reader less familiar with these tales, I have prepared brief introductions to the myths underlying each play and appended a glossary. Where the translation makes an important but indirect allusion to a character or place, I have noted at the foot of the page the glossary entry under which the information can be found. Sometimes, of course, ancient writers made statements or allusions which were probably as obscure to their contemporaries as they are to us, and were probably intended to puzzle or stimulate thought. These questions I have not attempted to answer in the text, but have left for the reader or performer to resolve.

A play, let us remind ourselves, is like a musical score in that it does not really live until it is performed. And then it has as many potentially different forms as it has directors, actors, and critics. So in the individual introductions to the plays I have sketched some questions the reader may want to ask about the characters and their roles. Characters in good drama, as in real life, are not simply linear, consistent beings (as scholars sometimes try to make them). They behave differently in different situations. They contradict themselves, they are often torn between conflicting impulses and obligations. Senecan drama is much more firmly rooted in the conflicts within the individual mind than are most Greek tragedies. Understanding the characters and the play involves a search for those areas or—to use a geological metaphor—those faults where different segments of a personality threaten each other and, in a larger sense, the stability of the world about them.

The Latin texts of the tragedies used are, in general, those of Elaine Fantham (*Seneca's "Troades": A Literary Introduction with Text, Translation, and Commentary*, [Princeton, 1982]), C. D. N. Costa, (Seneca, *Medea* [Oxford, 1973]), and P. Grimal (*L. Annaei Senecae Phaedra*, Erasme, Collection de textes latins commentés 14 [Paris, 1965]). I am grateful to Wolfgang Haase and the de Gruyter Press for giving me permission to reuse a few pages of my article "The Rider and the Horse: Politics and Power in Roman Poetry from Horace to Statius," *Aufstieg und Niedergang der römischen Welt* 32.1 (Berlin/New York, 1984), pp. 40–110. And I owe many debts to the friends and scholars who have given me advice and criticism: John Fitch, Eleanor Winsor Leach, Elaine Fantham, David Konstan, Joan Jeffri, David Keller, Rajani Sudan, and to my classics students and colleagues at Cornell, the University of Otago in New Zealand, and the University of Texas at Austin who helped me stage them. Sincere thanks also go to Martha Linke and Georgia Nugent, who saved me from many errors; my fellow editors of the Masters of Latin Literature, Diskin Clay, Douglass Parker, and Jon Stallworthy; above all, to my wife, Mary.

TROJAN WOMEN

Introduction to *Trojan Women*

Trojan Women has two major predecessors among surviving Greek tragedies both by Euripides: *Trojan Women* and *Hecuba*. Seneca's play differs significantly from both.

Play and Myth

The Greeks fought a ten-year war at Troy to recapture Helen, the wife of Menelaus, king of Sparta. Helen was abducted by Paris, one of the sons of Priam, king of Troy, and his wife, Hecuba. Under the leadership of Menelaus' brother Agamemnon, a fleet of a thousand ships gathered at Aulis in Boeotia for the invasion of Troy's territory. The fleet could not sail, however, because of adverse winds. The leaders therefore consulted Calchas, the chief prophet and holy man associated with the expedition, to discover how to obtain favoring winds. Calchas responded that the gods could be appeased only by human sacrifice—by the death of Agamemnon's own daughter, Iphigenia. Agamemnon consented. Thus the Trojan expedition ironically began with the sacrifice of an innocent child so that a wife of somewhat dubious morality could be retrieved.

During the Trojan War the chief warriors had been, on the Trojan side, Hector, another son of Priam and Hecuba, and on the Greek

---

For further reading, see Elaine Fanthan, ed., *Seneca's "Troades": A Literary Introduction with Text, Translation, and Commentary* (Princeton, 1982), and Marcus Wilson, "Seneca's *Agamemnon* and *Troades*" (dissertation, Monash University, Australia, 1985).

side Achilles, son of Peleus and the sea goddess Thetis. Hector is almost universally represented in ancient literature as an honorable warrior, the loyal child of Priam and defender of Troy, the loving husband of Andromache and devoted father to the infant Astyanax. Achilles, in contrast, is hot-tempered and petulant. Homer's *Iliad* tells of his famous quarrel with his commander in chief, Agamemnon, over a captive girl, Briseis, whom Agamemnon seized from Achilles. Slighted and insulted by his overlord, Achilles withdrew from the fighting, and Hector had his time of glory, almost reducing the Greeks to total defeat. Eventually Achilles relented enough to allow his friend Patroclus to wear his armor and go into battle to restore Greek morale. But Hector killed Patroclus. Mad with grief, Achilles rejoined the battle and killed Hector. Shortly afterward Achilles was himself killed by an arrow shot by Paris.

His death at the hands of a lesser warrior diminishes Achilles as a symbol of manliness and prowess. He was also diminished in the minds of his enemies by the fact that his mother had tried to prevent him from joining the Greek expedition against Troy in the first place. Thetis knew that if she could keep him from war he would live on to a ripe old age, but that if he went to war he would die young. So she disguised her son and raised him as a girl on the island of Scyros. But Achilles betrayed his masculinity in two ways. He fell in love with a young woman, Deidamia, and raped her. The child fathered by that rape was Pyrrhus (sometimes known as Neoptolemus). Although the rape was kept secret for some time, Achilles was eventually tricked into disclosing his masculine identity. A particularly cunning Greek prince, Ulysses (Odysseus), was sent to find him. Ulysses lured Achilles from hiding by bringing, among other gifts for the girls on Scyros, a sword. Achilles' fascination with the sword betrayed his identity to Ulysses.

After Hector and Achilles died, Achilles' son Pyrrhus joined the Greek forces at Troy. On the night Troy fell, Pyrrhus went on a rampage of slaughter, killing, among others, the old king Priam, who had sought sanctuary at an altar. As our play opens, all the male nobility of Troy, apart from Hector's son Astyanax, are dead or gone.[1] Only

---

[1] Seneca does not focus on the male adult survivors of Troy: Anchises, Aeneas, Antenor, and others who either betrayed Troy to the Greeks or simply escaped abroad,

the women are here; grieving, clustered together, they prepare for the degradation and slavery they know awaits them.

Notes and Questions about the Characters

Hecuba   Hecuba has the first and last words among the Trojan women. She is symbolic not only of what is left of Troy but, as she herself makes clear in her opening speech, of the fragility of royal power. She, the queen of a defeated country, clings—as does Andromache—to her residual sense of power and authority. She orchestrates the lamentations of the Trojan women as she once ruled their lives. No one has suffered as I have; everyone's sufferings are my sufferings; I am the queen of sorrows. Even when she discovers that in the lottery of captive women she is given as slave to Ulysses, most hated of the Greeks, she takes consolation in the fact that she has thus deprived him of the chance of an appealing woman; and in her last speech she takes a curiously pitiful pride in her survival: death was afraid of her.

Is she simply engaging in megalomaniacal self-justification for her personal survival amid universal catastrophe? Or is there something more to her attitude? Notice how outspokenly sarcastic she is with the Greeks, particularly with Pyrrhus when he comes to take Polyxena off to her death. She certainly challenges death and those who dispense it.

Andromache   Andromache is a complex and, I feel, disturbing character whose identity has, ultimately, one focal point: her dead husband, Hector. She participates with Ulysses in one of the greatest scenes from ancient drama, a chillingly "modern" scene of interrogation and psychological warfare. She tries to hide her son Astyanax from the Greeks by placing him in Hector's tomb and is eventually pressured by Ulysses into revealing his hiding place. (Why, incidentally, does it take her so long to realize that if Hector's tomb is

---

depending on which Greek or Roman source you read. The omission would not have gone unnoticed by Roman readers because of their familiarity with the tradition, enshrined in Vergil's *Aeneid*, that Aeneas went on to Italy, where he founded the Roman race.

37

demolished, Astyanax, who is in it, will be destroyed?) Modern readers tend to treat this passage as a kind of Gestapo scene pitting the fiendish interrogator against the helpless woman and her child. But to what extent is Ulysses actually correct in seeing that Andromache's aim is to preserve her son not for his own sake but because he is like Hector and because he may avenge Troy? And note Andromache's final action: she kisses her son's cloak in case any trace of Hector's ashes remains there. Andromache claims in her first scene that Astyanax is the only thing that keeps her from dying—she almost seems to resent the burden he places upon her. But does she go on to contemplate suicide when Astyanax is taken from her?

Agamemnon Agamemnon is pompous, condescending, and, in a grim way, funny. In his argument with Pyrrhus, is his prime concern to escape personal responsibility for any awful acts committed in the war? (He blames the sword and the dark of night for the total devastation that befell Troy.) Is this why Agamemnon defers to the priest Calchas, when backed into a corner (if he really is backed into a corner) by Pyrrhus, who is outraged that Agamemnon does not want to sacrifice Polyxena on Achilles' grave? Calchas not only unhesitatingly endorses Polyxena's death, but demands that of Astyanax as well.

That Agamemnon should now be so scrupulous about sacrificing Polyxena when at the beginning of the war (and also at Calchas' insistence) he sacrificed his own equally innocent daughter (and on the same pretext: that she was to be the bride of Achilles) seems preposterous to Pyrrhus. Is it? Who has created the precedent, Agamemnon or Calchas? Again and again in *Trojan Women* (as at the Nuremburg trials at the end of World War II) the issue is raised as to who is responsible for an atrocity: the person who orders it done or the person who carries out the order. Agamemnon (like Helen) seeks refuge in the notion that the person who gives the order, not the agent of the crime, is guilty.

Pyrrhus Pyrrhus makes no pretense that his actions are moral or need moral justification. Might is right; victory and defeat are the measures of justice and injustice. He glories in killing and especially in his father's actions. (He takes particular pleasure in describing men killed before the eyes of parents or other relatives.) Pyrrhus tires of arguing with Agamemnon and of the ludicrous personal abuse into which their interview dissolves; he gains his point when Agamemnon suddenly backs off and calls on Calchas to decide this issue. I have suggested in the stage directions that Pyrrhus may actually threaten Agamemnon at this point. Are there other viable dramatic alternatives?

Ulysses Ulysses is a horrifyingly subtle observer of others' behavior and knows how to manipulate by false friendliness and candor, logical persuasion, and—if he thinks it will work—terror. He adopts any persona or pose that suits his purpose at a given time. At one moment he will say that he is involved now only because he drew the lot to take Hector's son; soon after, however, he suggests that killing Astyanax is the proper course of action even from his own personal point of view. For this reason I think it is important for an actor to let Ulysses *seem* sympathetic to Andromache when his pose is one of sympathy, to make him more of a reluctant civil servant than a sinister member of the secret police. Ulysses combines candor about his purpose in coming to Andromache with lies about what his instructions were. He claims that Calchas had an alternative plan to gain a favorable departure from Troy in the event that Astyanax could not be taken alive: the destruction of Hector's tomb. Is this claim likely to be true? And does he really intend to destroy Hector's tomb? (Can we tell when he realizes that Astyanax is probably in the tomb?)

Helen Some critics see Helen as a sympathetic character, caught between her Greekness and her sympathy for Troy. Others see her as a fraud. Are not both views correct? Surely the real issue is the difference between the way Helen sees herself and the way others see her. She has to cope with public contempt and scorn as Hecuba must cope with loss of power. She rationalizes. In her opening soliloquy she seems almost humorously self-critical. But she does fall back on the old argument that guilt for a crime lies with the person who orders it done, not with the agent of the order. Similarly, Helen claims she is worse off than the other captive women because they do not yet know who their masters will be, whereas she knows she must be given over to Menelaus. Accept her logic if you will. But do note that Helen herself knows and tells (with perhaps a touch of Laconic satisfaction) the results of the lottery which will assign each Trojan woman a master.

Calchas   A brief but vital role. The part, I think, will play better if Calchas is on stage throughout the dialogue between Pyrrhus and Agamemnon. Such staging would conform well with other powerful uses of mute (or almost mute) characters in this play. Astyanax is the center of attention but says only "Pity me, mother" (and notice that he asks her, not Ulysses, to pity him). Similarly, Polyxena is the center of attention as Helen comes on to get her. She is spoken to but never speaks. Likewise, when Pyrrhus enters to escort Polyxena to her death, he does not speak but is addressed (and mocked) by Hecuba.

The Old Servant   This character was almost certainly intended to be male, but would play quite well as female. One of the tricky decisions in staging the play is how and when to get him (or her) offstage. Is the Old Servant suggesting to Andromache that she ought to kill him (her)?

Talthybius   The manuscripts give Talthybius only the first messenger speech and assign the second to a nameless "messenger." There is no satisfactory reason not to combine the roles. Indeed, an intriguing and obviously Greek character emerges from such a blend. He maintains an aura of sympathy toward the Trojan women and morally condemns the actions of the Greeks. Why? Could it be that his is the play's final act of treachery, since he has the very last lines and uses them to reiterate the theme of callousness, hurrying the captives along as the fleet is moving out? The only male character who might take an unwavering moral stand proves no less hypocritical than the others. As Ulysses will tolerate Andromache's tears only briefly for fear of delaying departure, so Talthybius will not allow reaction to his message of sorrow to hold up the deportation indefinitely.

CHARACTERS

HECUBA	queen of Troy; widow of Priam; mother of Hector and Paris; mother-in-law of Andromache
TALTHYBIUS	Greek messenger
AGAMEMNON	king of Mycenae; commander in chief of the Greek expedition against Troy
PYRRHUS	son of Achilles and killer of Hecuba's husband, Priam
CALCHAS	Greek priest
ANDROMACHE	daughter-in-law of Hecuba; widow of Hector
OLD SERVANT	attendant of Andromache
ASTYANAX	son of Andromache and Hector
ULYSSES	king of Ithaca; Greek commander at Troy
HELEN	wife of the Greek king, Menelaus; eloped with Hecuba's son Paris

POLYXENA (nonspeaking) daughter of Hecuba; sister of Andromache

CHORUS OF TROJAN WOMEN

VARIOUS ATTENDANTS (nonspeaking)

ACT I

*Scene: Somewhere outside the ruined city of Troy, just before dawn. The set
should suggest the total and recent devastation which has left only one tower in
the city fortifications still standing. Fires still burn in the city. Huddled in groups
around the stage are Trojan women, sitting in dazed silence. Among them are
HECUBA and her daughters, POLYXENA and CASSANDRA. They are dressed
in the tatters of once elegant gowns.*

*HECUBA, queen of Troy, a woman in early old age, is awake, reflecting
on her own and her city's fate. She addresses her thoughts to the audience,
conscious somehow that posterity will be watching her.*

Hecuba:	You are a king, confident in your power,
	lord and master in your palace walls.
	Heaven turn its back on you? Oh no,
	your luck has been so good you must believe
	in it.
	Now look at me, at Troy. Mankind's
	proud pedestals, how easily they're smashed.
	History offers no greater proof than us:
	the pillar of Asia, toppled and broken
	though gods came flocking once to raise it up.
	Kings rallied to defend it: a blond hero
	who drank from where the icy Don opens
	its bite of seven mouths; a dark hero,
	who mingled tepid Tigris with the red,
	salt Gulf, always first to pluck the day
	new from its birthbed while we others slept.
	A heroine too, neighbor of nomad Scyths.

10

---

a blond hero: Rhesus
a dark hero: Memnon
a heroine: Penthesilea

Around the Black Sea, with no man among
her warriors, she struck men mad with fear.

Now Troy's struck down and, like a hero's ghost,
hovers above its tomb.
              The wall, its tall
and lovely parapets, lie dead and burned
and dense with shattered roofs, not crowds of men.
Only fires now court the palace; smoke
issues from the home of Trojan kings.
Yet searing flames do not deter greedy,
victorious hands. They plunder while Troy burns.
Waves of smoke disguise the heavens, clouds
raven and putrid with ash from Troy   20
blot out the sun. Our conquerors, although
they hunger for revenge, stop still—fierce eyes
measure Ilium's slow fall: ten years,
and finally forgiveness forged in fire.
Troy awes them as she burns. Although
they longed for, and now see before their eyes,
Troy ash-deep and forsaken, they cannot
believe they could have forced her down. And yet,
they ravage her. A thousand ships lack space
for all the spoils.

              The gods hate me, but still
they'll bear me out. So will my home's burned bones,
and Priam, king of Troy, who's buried now—
the whole city his grave. So will your ghost,   30
Hector. While you stood, Troy stood. All
my great flocks of children, countless, lesser
shades, you too will be my witnesses.
When mad, inspired Cassandra prophesied
catastrophe, no one believed her though
she was Phoebus' priestess of prophecy;
her god would not let anyone believe.
But I foresaw it all before she did,
I, Hecuba, with the frightened insight

of a mother-to-be. I dreamed a torch
of fire, and not a son, was in my womb.
I didn't keep this knowledge to myself.
I told them all. And they all ridiculed
my prophecies before they ridiculed
Cassandra.

No, it was not Ulysses,
cunning man, or his night-prowling friend,
Diomedes, who threw the blazing fires
among you; it was not the liar Sinon
and the wooden horse. I lit Troy's fires.
The city burns, you burn, with flames kindled
inside my womb.
(HECUBA *cuts in her own reverie.*)

What is it, Hecuba?   40
You're an old woman, still clinging to life.
Why cry over a city dead and gone?
You've sorrows, losses, more immediate.
The fall of Troy is history.
(HECUBA *pauses before resuming her thoughts.*)

I saw
that crime—no, an abominable sin
it was, not crime—the murder of a king
upon the very altar where he fled
for sanctuary.

There Achilles' son
seized Priam by the hair, with his left hand
twisting it right round and forcing back
the old man's head, plunging ungodly sword
hilt-deep in Priam's throat, so brutishly
relishing the killing of a king
so old and drained of life that when the sword
was wrenched out it displayed no spot of blood.
He was already old and close to death.   50
Knowing this, who would not know enough
to let plain nature take its course?

A sin
this was, committed before heaven's eyes,

45

before whatever holy power lurks
still in a dead kingdom. Many kings
you fathered, Priam, but you have no tomb.
Your body has no pyre. And Troy's burning!
Enough? Not for the powers above! Right now
a democratic lottery's being held
to part the plunder fairly. So daughters,
daughters-in-law of Priam's house, and I,
unvalued prize of war, will find a lord.
Someone's pledging himself to Hector's wife.
Someone wants Helenus' wife, or Antenor's.   60
There's one who wants to crawl into your bed,
Cassandra. Yes, their only fear is this:
that I will be their prize. For I am now
the only thing that terrifies the Greeks.

Why have you stopped your crying, prisoners,
my fellow prisoners? Beat your breasts,
shriek your laments, sing requiem for Troy.
Ida, accursed mountain where Paris
passed fatal judgment, should certainly
be echoing by now your cries of grief.

(*The women, wakened by* HECUBA'*s exhortation, stir from
their vigil and silence. They speak, either in unison or
separately.*)

Chorus: You tell us to cry, but we know, we know—
for ten long years we've sobbed and wept—
ever since Phrygian Paris sailed to Sparta,   70
cutting the waves in the boat of pinewood
sacred to Troy's mother earth—
Ten times Mount Ida aged with snow—
ten times her forests have been stripped
to burn our dead—
ten times the farmer on the plain of Sigeum

---

mother earth: Cybele

shuddered with fear as sickle
reaped harvest—

Not a day has passed when we have not wept—
but now fate serves us
yet another cause for tears—
So we will weep
and sing our threnody—
Raise your hand, my queen, and we
will follow in sadness;
our cheap lives will follow their mistress—   80
It is not hard to teach us grief.

Hecuba: Trusted companions of my fall,
untie the ribbons in your hair,
and let it blow free around your necks,
sad and filthy with ash of Troy.
Fill your hands with the dust!
That's all of Troy that's left to us.

Open your dresses, bare your arms,
knot the sleeves around your thighs,
let your legs give open access to your wombs.
There is no chastity when you're a slave;
you wear a veil for marriage,   90
not for rape.

Now your skirts are loosened, tie them with your
        shawls,
keep your hands free so they can
lash you in mad rhythms of grief.
Now that's how you should look,
that's the way. Now you're Trojan women
I can recognize.

Back to the past;
let us weep for the past,
let us weep for the past more bitterly

than ever before.
Let us weep for Hector.

Chorus: We've untied the ribbons on our heads—
as we have done at countless funerals—
Our hair blows free—
Troy's hot ashes   100
spatter our faces—

Our shoulders are bare—
our dresses fall
till only our thighs
are covered by their folds—

Our breasts are naked
and await our blows—

Now will our sorrow pour forth all its strength!—
Now let the farthest seashores of our land
resound our moans of grief.
Let echoing mountain hollows
shriek back our cries of sorrow
in full chorus—
not just the short, quick echo
of our final words—   110

The depths of sea—
the heights of heavens—
must hear our cry—
Hands, bruise my breast,
make it throb with savage blows
louder and deeper than ever before!—
Hector, we weep for you.

Hecuba: For you, Hector, hands rip shoulders,
gash arms till they are red with blood.
For you, fists smash against heads;
for you, a mother's breasts   120

are scarred by her own nails.
I reopen every wound I made
the day we buried you.
They must redden and flow with blood and blood.

Pillar of Troy, Delayer of doom,
Protector of the tired Phrygian people,
you were our fortress.
Ten years Troy stood,
propped on your mighty shoulders.
Then she fell with you the day you died.
Your last day, Hector, was her last day too.

Now let us lament Priam in our dirge of sorrow.   130
Enough for Hector.

Chorus: Ruler of Phrygia, hear our cries—
Take this tribute of our tears—
Twice you were taken prisoner—
Twice Troy's walls were shattered by Greek steel—
Twice Hercules' quivers
were emptied into our bodies—
When you were king
nothing happened just once.

Then Hecuba's children, son by son,
were carried to their graves—
kings, flocking like sheep to slaughter—
And after all their funerals, you came—
their father, final victim
of the lord of heaven—
Sprawled on the shores of Sigeum,   140
hacked down and headless.

Hecuba: Save your tears for other deaths,
women of Troy, don't waste

---

hacked down and headless: see Pompey

pity on my Priam.
"Priam has every fruit of happiness,"
let this be your cry.
He died a free man.
Proudly he walks down among the ghosts.
He'll never wear a Greek slave's iron collar,
he does not have to watch Atreus' twin sons,
or look out for
treacherous Ulysses.
He will never be part of their spoils,   150
his head bowed down, a symbol
of their victory.

Those hands that once wielded the scepter's power
will not be pinned behind his back;
he'll never follow Agamemnon's chariot,
handcuffed in gold,
paraded through the wide streets of Mycenae.

Chorus: "Priam has every fruit of happiness":
We all say this—
for when he died, he took his kingdom with him—
and now he roams in safety
through the shaded gardens of paradise—
among the ghosts of good men—   160
looking for Hector—

"Priam has every fruit of happiness"—
Fruitful and happy is anyone who dies in war
and, as he dies,
takes everything with him.

ACT II

Enter TALTHYBIUS, *a Greek Messenger.*

Talthybius: The sons of Danaus are always doomed,
it seems, to deadly delays in port
whether they're heading for a fight, or home.

Chorus: What cause could possibly create delay
for ships, Danaan ships at that? Tell us
what god has closed the path that leads you home.

Talthybius: My mind and limbs shiver and quiver, struck
with horror. Yet to believe something
so hideous it transcends the truth is hard.
But I saw it, saw it with my own eyes.

Sun's rays grazed mountain peaks as he arose;   170
day had defeated night. A bull-like roar—
who knows where from—was on us in a flash.
The earth shook, violently heaving up
each layer of rock from its most hidden folds.
Trees shook their heads, and towering forests
thundered the sound of timber split apart.
Not even Holy Woods were spared. Ripped
from Ida's ridges, rock masses cascade.
No mere earth tremor this. Sea sensed it too,
sensed its son Achilles near at hand,
waved watery carpets up onto the beach.

---

delays in port: see Aulis

A huge chasm rent the valley floor,
creating vast caves, jaws of an abyss
plunging down to Hell, making a path   180
upward for the dead through shattered earth,
raising Achilles' tomb. The hero's ghost
shone forth like a beam of light, as huge
as when he fought the warriors of Thrace
while limbering up for the attack on Troy.

Do you remember when he killed Cygnus,
Neptune's son who gleamed with swan-white hair?
When war was at its height, and he himself
was at the height of war's fury? Recall
how he choked the Xanthus estuary
with dams of corpses, how the river spilled
bloody waters over banks, trying
to reach the sea? Recall his hour of pride
when, towering high in his chariot,
he held the reins and dragged Hector and Troy
behind him in the dust?
                        This was the same
Achilles that I saw, and every beach
filled with the roaring of his angry voice: 190
"Sail, idle creatures, sail! Pay me the debt
you owe my mighty ghost. Thankless creatures,
I'm son of the sea, it's my waters
you will be traveling. You once paid
a dread price for my anger, Greece. You'll pay
again. I want a bride to share my tomb.
I want Polyxena, my promised prize.
Pyrrhus' hand will slaughter her; her blood
will quench my grave's yearning."
                        He cried these words,
shattering the brilliant day with dark
profound. Returning then to Death's embrace

Death: Dis

he thrust himself into the cavernous
vastness; earth closed up and held him tight.
Threatening winds subside; the now calm sea   200
sighs, motionless and dead, with gentle heave
of waves; and spirits, fathoms-deep, sing high
their seashell wedding hymn for bride and groom.

(*Exit* TALTHYBIUS, *the* CHORUS, *and* HECUBA. *The scene
now changes to Agamemnon's tent.* AGAMEMNON *is sitting
at a table or walking about, listening as* PYRRHUS *rails at
him. Behind them, back to the audience, is* CALCHAS.)

Pyrrhus: You were in high spirits about leaving,
ready to sail home. Achilles was just
forgotten. You did not recall that he
alone defeated Troy; the sole reason
the city did not fall the moment he
was dead was that she didn't know which way
to fall.
        Suppose you wanted to give him
what he asks, and give it quickly, you'd
be too late. Your senior officers
have already made off with his fair share.

He was man at his best; he'd earned his prize.
You couldn't pay him any less than this.   210

He was warned to run away from war,
told he should sit at home and live his life
to ripe old age—more years than old Nestor.
His mother even tried, with some success,
to hide him away, disguising him
as a girl. He threw off this pretense.
He chose the sword. He proved he was a man.

---

spirits: Triton(s)
his arms had power: see Telephus
His mother: Thetis

King Telephus, a formidable foe,
detested strangers. He denied access
into his fierce country. So Achilles,
though a raw beginner, steeped his hands
in that king's blood, and only then perceived
his arms had power to cure as well as kill.
Next Thebes fell. Andromache's father
found his kingdom conquered, and himself
a prisoner. The same fate undermined   220
Lyrnesos too—a minor city, true,
but highly placed atop a chain of hills.
Likewise the land famous for Briseis,
the captive girl he loved. Likewise Chryse,
your girlfriend's home. And what a history
of quarrels came with that. Next Tenedos—
famous in its own way, fertile Scyros,
flocking with sheep, and Lesbos, bisecting
the Aegean. Then Cilla, a place
that Phoebus loves.

              You know the Caycus,
roaring high in springtime flood? Each town
its waters lap my father washed away.
The nations he wiped out, the stark terror
he caused, so many towns shattered as if
by a tornado of astounding force:
glory's pinnacle such deeds would be   230
for any other man; for Achilles
just steps along the way. Yes, that is how
my father came to Troy. He fought these wars
to train himself for war.

                  Forget all this.
Now wouldn't Hector's death have been enough,
all by itself?

           My father conquered Troy.
You tore it down.

              A great man, my father.
I like reliving the fine deeds he did,
the praise they won him: Hector lying dead,

killed before his father's eyes, Memnon,
before his uncle's. Memnon's mother, Dawn,
was so distressed her face paled into mourning   240
the next day.
                    Achilles shuddered too
at what his victory meant. Even the child
of a goddess, he learned, is doomed to die.

Penthesilea was the next to fall,
and with her your last real fear.
                              You owe
Achilles, if you reckon up your debts
correctly. If he were to want a girl
from your own city, you'd have to admit
that he deserved her.
                    Still unsure? You thought
this kind of thing all right a while ago.
Now disapproval in a sudden surge.
Is it too cruel, you think, to sacrifice
Priam's child to Peleus' child?
But you're a father too, and killed your child
for Helen's sake. So there's a precedent.
All I'm asking is the usual thing.

Agamemnon: Why do young people never keep some rein   250
         on passion? Now, with all the rest, age
         is the problem. The first fires of lust
         ravish their senses.
                         Not so with Pyrrhus.
         His father's his fetish.
                              In days gone by
         I patiently rode out Achilles' threats,
         his arrogance, his blustering, swollen pride.
         When you've a lot of power, you must take
         a lot of nonsense, and take it calmly.

Killed your child: see Aulis

Achilles earned distinction in the field;
his memory deserves honor. Why must
you spatter it with grisly butchery?
It would become you, Pyrrhus, as your first
lesson, to learn what limits should apply
to what a winner does, and what is done
to one who's lost. And no one who has ruled
by violence has ever ruled for long.
Restraint maintains your power. As Fortune lifts
you up, and as you reap rewards from life,   260
the more it then becomes you to control
yourself in your prosperity, to be
afraid when heaven is too good, shiver
at what might happen. I have won a war,
therefore I have learned greatness is toppled
in a flash. Does victory, does Troy
make us too savage and too proud? We stand,
we Danaans, upon the pinnacle
from which Troy fell.
                      Now I admit my power
has, on occasion, shaped the way I rule:
I've carried my head a little higher
than I ought. But, then, experience
of fortune's ups and downs has smashed these grand
illusions in me though it would have spurred
their growth in other men. You made me proud,
Priam. You also frighten me. How can   270
I now think of sovereignty as more
than a mere name, gilded with false glitter—
hair decorated with what really is
a chain of gold?
                Some quick calamity
will snatch it all away. It doesn't take
a thousand ships, it doesn't always take
ten years. Misfortune doesn't hover over
everyone. It's not always so slow.

You made me proud: because I conquered you

I will admit, and I say this without,
I hope, offending you, my dear homeland:
I wanted Troy to suffer and to fall.
I wish, however, I had had the power
to stop it being razed down to the ground.
But the forces of anger could not be
reined in; the enemy burned to resist,
and victory was won at dead of night.   280
If anything happened which might be thought
an outrage, or just inappropriate,
blame it on anger, blame it on the dark,
when passion fires itself spontaneously.
And blame the sword. When it achieves results,
once it has tasted blood, the sword is seized
by an insatiable desire for more.

What parts of Troy withstood the holocaust
should be allowed to stand. Reparation
has been made—enough, more than enough.
Indeed, I will not tolerate the thought
that a king's daughter should be sacrificed
in funeral offering, or that her blood
should drench some ashes. I will not permit
atrocious slaughter of this kind to be
graced with the name of marriage.

                               And, besides,
I'll get all the blame. A man who fails
to stop a crime, although he has the power,   290
orders the execution of that crime.

Pyrrhus: Achilles' ghost will get no tribute, then?

Agamemnon: Of course it will. The world will sing his praise,
the unknown corners of the earth will know
his glory and his name. If pouring blood
upon his ashes makes his being dead
easier to endure, then we'll slit throats

57

prime throats of flocking oxen, not Troy's kings.
No mother's tears must fall for blood we shed.
If we take human life when humans die,
what precedents are set? Besides, you'll bring
hatred and loathing on your father's name.
You're mixing up his cult with punishment
for him, not just for her. So spare him this.   300

Pyrrhus: You may be all fire when everything
goes your way, raising your self-esteem.
But you're all fear when leaves crackle at night.
You're tyrant over kings, not king of kings.
(*Remembering how Agamemnon once quarreled with Achilles
about a woman,* PYRRHUS *suddenly and nastily suggests Agamemnon may want Polyxena for himself.*)
Burning with love again, Agamemnon?
Your lust is tickled by this newfound girl?
How often will you take what we have won
and keep it for yourself? My hand will see
Achilles gets due rights of conquest. So,
if you refuse, if you hang on to her,
I'll send a rather bigger sacrifice,
the kind Pyrrhus should send. It's far too long
since I last killed a king. Priam demands
a worthy match.

Agamemnon   I would never deny   310
that this was Pyrrhus' finest hour in war.
Your father pitied Priam when he begged
for mercy. Now he's dead. And you hacked him
to pieces with your sword.

Pyrrhus: All those who begged
my father's pity were his enemies.
That much I've learned. Priam, at least, had guts
enough to beg in person. But when you
needed him, you were witless with fear,
you didn't even dare to come and beg.
Ulysses and Ajax were sent to do

your praying for you. You shut yourself
away, in terror of your enemy.

Agamemnon: Your father, I admit, was not afraid
on *that* occasion. While the ships were burned
and Greeks were being slaughtered, he played dead,
stretched idly on his back. War and combat
were far from his mind, and he just strummed   320
his lilting, tortoise lyre with lightweight pick.

Pyrrhus: Hector, on that occasion, didn't give
a damn about your sword. Achilles' song,
however, terrified him. Though a ring
of panic held you in its grip, nothing
disturbed the peace profound among our ships
from Thessaly.

Agamemnon: No doubt the same profound
peace dead Hector's father later found
among your ships from Thessaly.

Pyrrhus: A man
profoundly a king will spare a king.

Agamemnon: Then why did you rob Priam of his life?

Pyrrhus: If you're truly sorry for someone,
you'll often grant death rather than life.

Agamemnon: I see. You're truly sorry for the girl,
that's why you want to kill her on the grave?

Pyrrhus: So . . . nowadays you think it is a sin
to use a girl for human sacrifice?   330

Agamemnon: It is becoming for a king to put
his fatherland before his own children.

Pyrrhus: No law says I must spare a prisoner.
                 No law declares that I can't punish them.

Agamemnon: No law. Only honor and decency.

Pyrrhus: Winning grants license for what we desire.

Agamemnon: The more license we have for our desires,
                 the less it is becoming to indulge.

Pyrrhus: You dare say that, you? Ten years you choked
                 our troops with tyranny. Pyrrhus freed them.

Agamemnon: Do you get this courage from your girls
                 in Scyros?

Pyrrhus: (*interrupting*) Well, we don't get it the way
                 your family does, by eating human flesh.

Agamemnon: (*continuing as if no interruption has occurred*)
                 Cut off from men by waves . . .

Pyrrhus: They are the waves   340
                 of my ancestral sea. I've heard about
                 your famous parentage: Atreus' House,
                 or was it Thyestes'?

Agamemnon: But your mother
                 conceived you from Achilles as a girl,
                 too young for marriage, not too young for rape.
                 They kept things rather quiet, didn't they?
                 But then, of course, he wasn't yet a man.

Pyrrhus: From famous Achilles, whose lineage,
                 distributed about the universe
                 includes all provinces of heavenly power:

---

not too young for rape: see Achilles

in Thetis, the Sea; in Aeacus,
the Dead; the Sky in Jupiter.

Agamemnon: Famous
Achilles? You mean the one that Paris killed?

Pyrrhus: I mean the one no single god would dare
to meet in combat, fighting hand to hand . . .
(PYRRHUS *moves his hand toward his sword, menacingly.*)

Agamemnon: I could stop your big talk once and for all,
ruthlessly taming all your arrogance.
But my sword knows mercy even for those   350
who are within my power.
                    Let's ask Calchas
instead. He knows god's will. And if god's will
demands her death, then I will grant it you.
(CALCHAS, *who has until now been standing silent and motionless, with his back to the audience, turns around and moves
towards the front of the stage.*)
Ah, Calchas! When our ships were all tied up
in Greece, and could not leave, you cut us loose,
showing how we could end deadly delays.
Your skill unlocks the sky, finds hidden signs
growing in animal innards. Thunder
and lightning give you insight into fate.
So does the comet dragging its long tail
of fire. Your words have always cost me dear.
But speak for fate. Tell us what god commands.
Calchas, in counsel you must be my king.

Calchas: The Greeks are granted sailing by the fates,   360
and at the usual price: a young virgin
must be honored as an offering
to the King of Thessaly, and on
his funeral mound, dressed in the usual

---

cost me dear: see Aulis

wedding gown for brides of Thessaly—
Mycenaean or Ionian,
if you prefer. Pyrrhus should give away
the bride. Her "giving," thus, will be both right
and ritual.
           Oh, one more thing: she's not
the only cause that's holding back our ships.
Blood better known than yours is owed to god,
Polyxena. He whom the fates require
should fall from a high tower and meet his death.
He is grandson of Priam, Hector's son:
Astyanax. Once this is done, the fleet
can fill the sea with all its thousand sails.   370

(CALCHAS *escorts* AGAMEMNON *and* PYRRHUS *offstage.*
The former adversaries are now reconciled. The scene shifts
back to Hector's tomb. The CHORUS *reenters somberly and*
slowly.)

Chorus: They say the soul lives on when we are dead—
Can this be true, or is it just a myth,
an opiate to dull our fears?
When one who loves us shuts our eyes in death—
on that last day without daylight—
when ashes are sealed in the urn—
do we live on, poor creatures,
can we not wholly consign
our being to the grave?—
Or then again—
is death complete and absolute,
does not one fragment of our life live on,
does soul flee, like a puff of air,
up into sky, mingled forever with clouds
when we take final breath,
when the cremating flames lick naked thighs?—   380

Sun rises, travels the world before he sets—
Ocean's blue waters lap every shore

in ebb and flow—
And everything Sun and Sea behold
scurries to doom, dragged by time,
soaring swift as Pegasus—

Cosmic winds ceaselessly whirl the zodiac—
Mighty Sun, king of galaxies,
as he rotates, spins on centuries—
Each night bewitching moon
in arching orbit
skimming skies,
follows the plan of Destiny—

And so do we—

Then, when we reach Hell's swirling streams,
the Styx, the ultimate boundary of truth,   390
binding oaths of gods irrevocably,
we cease to be, exist no more—
Like smoke from a hot fire,
we briefly soil the air,
then vanish and disperse to nothingness—

The souls ruling our bodies,
like rainclouds drifting in sky,
suddenly scatter in cold north wind,
gone traceless in vastness—

Nothing exists after death,
and death is not a state—
only the end of the final lap
of fleeting life—

Greedy men, stop hoping for reward—
Anxious men, stop fearing punishment—
Time's rapacious jaws devour us whole—   400

Death cannot be divided:
it destroys the body,
does not spare the soul—

There is no Hell, no savage god who rules the dead,
no guardian dog to hinder your escape—
These are just idle folktales, empty words,
myth, woven into nightmare—

"Where will I lie when I am dead?" you ask—

You will lie among things never born.

ACT III

Enter ANDROMACHE, *accompanied by an* OLD SERVANT, *and by her son,* ASTYANAX.

Andromache: Why tear hair and beat breasts in your sorrow,
women of Troy? Why drench your cheeks with tears?
What we have suffered must be trivial   410
if it is something we can cry about.
For you the fall of Troy was yesterday;
for me Troy died long since, when Achilles
lashed his chariot, axle shuddering
with the weight of Hector's corpse. That day
my limbs were dragged in dust, that day I died.
That's when Troy fell. Now I am rigidly
impervious to horror, I absorb
each new blow and feel nothing. I'd have torn
myself from the Greeks' grasp, followed Hector,
had he (*indicating* ASTYANAX) not held me back. He
    tames that urge,
keeps me from death, keeps me praying to god,   420
prolongs my troubles.
              The chief benefit
of losing everything is the knowledge
that there is nothing left to fear. My son
deprives me of that benefit. All chance
of happiness is snatched away. But still
horror can crawl through. How pitiful:
to be afraid, when, if hope lingered on,
there'd be nothing to hope for anyway.

(*The* OLD SERVANT *motions the Chorus to depart, watches them go, then turns to* ANDROMACHE.)

Old Servant: What has occurred that frightens you and adds,
               suddenly, to your grief?

Andromache: From great evil
               a greater rises up. Dust settles still.
               Troy is still falling.

Old Servant: Suppose he wanted to:
               What further suffering *could* god devise?

Andromache: Death's gates fly open, caverns of the dead   430
               are now unlocked. Departed enemies
               part darkness' deepest pits to bring terror
               upon the conquered. Why can only Greeks
               return from death, egalitarian death?
               All Trojans tremble at Achilles' ghost;
               but my mind alone is stalked at night
               by the horror of that awful dream.

Old Servant: What dream? Tell me your fears now, openly.

Andromache: It was a soothing night—and two parts gone.
               I'd watched the Dipper's seven stars rotate
               until, some time between midnight and dawn,
               I fell asleep. I'd almost forgotten
               what rest was in my troubles. Now I felt
               my face relax.
                       The sleep was short—if sleep   440
               is the right word for that paralysis
               of mind that grips you when you're deep in shock.
               Suddenly Hector stood before my eyes—
               not the aggressive Hector who once torched
               Greek ships with fire from Ida, burning for
               indiscriminate slaughter, and clad
               in the real armor of Achilles, stripped
               from a false corpse.

---

from a false corpse: see Patroclus

The Hector that I saw
appeared dejected, tired; the usual fire
was missing from his eyes. He looked as though
he'd been crying—like me. His hair was all
unkempt and filthy. But just seeing him   450
was nice. He shook his head: "My faithful wife,"
he said. "Wake up! Take our child away.
This is our only chance. You must hide him.
Stop weeping! Are you moaning because Troy
is fallen? How I wish it were, quite dead.
Be quick, and take him anywhere you can!
Don't let this little branch be cut away."
I shook with icy terror; my trembling
woke me. I forgot my son. My eyes,
scanning the room in fear, searched for Hector.
But his ghost cheated me, slipped through my arms
as I embraced him.
(*to* ASTYANAX)   Oh my son, clearly   460
your father's son, you're Troy's last hope, the only
hope for our tormented family.
Your veins are filled with much too famous blood,
you are too like your father: for you have
my Hector's face, walk, manner, powerful hands,
even the frightening look he used to have
when he shook his head and tossed his hair.
You were born too late for Troy, my son,
but too soon for me. I wonder if
that glorious day will come when you'll defend   470
and avenge this soil of Troy, rebuild
our Pergamum, bring home its peoples, exiled
across the earth, and give the Phrygians
their homeland, their identity, again.

I've not forgotten where we stand. I fear
this is too much to ask. Let's pray for life,
that is one thing for which a prisoner
can surely pray.
                    Where can I hide you? Where

67

is safe enough that I won't be afraid?
Our city was once so powerful.
Gods gave it wealth, gods built its walls. The world
knew Troy; it was envied, and it was feared
by people everywhere. What is it now?
Skeletons and ashes charred by flames.   480
In the vast emptiness, nothing still stands
that's large enough to hide a tiny child.
Where can I put him so I'll cheat the Greeks?

Of course! Even the enemy respects
my dear husband's grave. Priam built it
grand in scale and cost. For in their grief
kings spare nothing.
                     That's what I'll do. It's best
to trust him to his father's keeping.
                                       Yet
cold sweat soaks my limbs. This is a place
of death. I shudder at what this forebodes.

Old Servant: Recall that many have been saved from death
because people believed that they were dead.

Andromache: There's no real hope. His great nobility   490
is now a massive weight which crushes him.
The danger of betrayal's very great.

Old Servant: Get rid of any witnesses.

                                       But if
Andromache: the enemy comes out in search of him?

Old Servant: Tell them he died while Troy was being sacked.

Andromache: And what's the point? He'll fall into their hands
eventually.

Gods gave it wealth: Neptune, Phoebus

68

Old Servant: But the conquerors
are always worst when victory is fresh.

Andromache: How can he hide without being afraid,
without my being afraid?

Old Servant: You have no choice.
Seize what protection you can find. When luck
goes, with it goes the luxury of choice.

Andromache: Is there a place on earth where no road leads,
so far away that you'll be safe? Who'll help?
Who'll protect us in our fear? Hector,
you've always guarded us. We are still yours,   500
so guard us now. I have been loyal to you,
I've stolen him away. Look after him.
We rely on you though you are dead.
Take him, so he can live.
(ANDROMACHE *kisses* ASTYANAX *and gives him to the*
OLD SERVANT *to conduct into the tomb.* ASTYANAX *shies
away.*)
                        Astyanax,
go on into the tomb, don't run away.
Don't be too proud to hide. Oh, you *are*
Hector's son, ashamed to display fear!
Courage was all right yesterday. Today,
you must take what is given. Look at me,
look at what's left of us: a grave, a child,
a prisoner. We've lost, we've got to yield.
Bring yourself to it! Now in you go,
into your father's tomb.
(*The* OLD SERVANT *guides* ASTYANAX *into the tomb.*)
                     Here you'll be safe,
if providence helps people in distress.   510
If not, you'll have a grave.
(ANDROMACHE *begins to weep.*)

Old Servant: He's safely in,
I've barred the entrance. To make sure your fear
does not betray him, get away from here
and stay away.

Andromache: You fear less when you're close.
(*The* OLD SERVANT *firmly moves to* ANDROMACHE *to
guide her away.*)
All right, if that's your will, I'll go away.

(*The* OLD SERVANT *stops in horror and looks offstage.*)
Old Servant: Quiet a moment! Stop crying at once!
Ulysses, that man whose name we curse,
is heading towards us now.

Andromache: Earth, open up.
Hector, tear the ground, rip it open
to the bottommost pit of Hell. Bury   520
what I have placed in trust with you beneath
the deepest waters of the dead. He's here.
There's hesitation in his walk. His mind
is shrewdly plotting something devious.

(*Enter* ULYSSES, *accompanied by a small group of soldiers.
The* OLD SERVANT, *if male, is either removed by the soldiers or, if female, may remain on stage with* ANDROMACHE
during the following scene. ULYSSES *observes and slowly ap-
proaches* ANDROMACHE.)

Ulysses: It is my task to bring unpleasant news.
So first, let me request just this of you:
you must believe that what you're going to hear
is my voice speaking someone else's words.
Believe that this decision isn't mine,
but the collective voice of High Command.
Our quest is for a chance to travel home;
we're overdue, and Hector's infant is

the obstacle that holds us back. So Fate
requests that we search out that obstacle.

The Greeks will always be troubled, and lack
confidence in peace because there is
no guarantee that it will last. They will
always be looking over their shoulders,   530
unable to disarm, Andromache,
while your son keeps up Trojan morale,
though Troy itself is crushed.
                                        This song Calchas,
our visionary, sings. Yet even if
Calchas, our visionary, had maintained
a tight-shut mouth, still Hector's precedent
gave constant warning we should take this course.
Even Hector's offspring frightens me.
The properties of seed, of thoroughbreds,
assert themselves. The small bull follows in
the large bull's steps, and though his horns have not
cut through the hide upon his head, he's there
quite unexpectedly, eyes raised, head high,
leading his father's herd: the overlord.   540

Hack down a tree. You'll see a tender shoot
sprout from the trunk. Give it a little time,
and it will grow tall as its mother plant.
Earth will be shaded once again; the gods
will have another holy grove.
                                        If you
are careless, fail to stamp on every trace
of ash, so rife after a major blaze,
there's fire again. The flames regain their strength.

You can't assess things justly when you feel
sorry for yourself. Think it over
in your heart, and you'll forgive the Greeks.
Ten years they've been here now, ten long summers

71

without a harvest. Aging and afraid,
the soldiers fear one more disastrous war,
they think that Troy will never be buried   550
totally. It's your Hector-to-be
that moves them to anxiety. So free
the Greeks from fear. Our ships are on the beach.
They're ready but, because of this, they're stuck.
Don't think me cruel in what I do. That's why
I'm here for Hector's son. I would have gone
for Agamemnon's child. And, by the way,
you're only suffering what he himself
had to endure as price of victory.

Andromache: Would you were in your mother's arms, my son.
I wish I knew what had befallen you,
what had snatched you from me—or where you were.
I'd never have betrayed you, forgotten
you were my child, not even if they'd carved
my heart out with swords, or shackled me
with chains that cut into my wrists, even
if fire surrounded me on every side.   560
Where are you now, my son? What's happening?
Perhaps you're lost and wandering aimlessly
over the fields. Perhaps your limbs are seared
in a vast cloud of devastating smoke
from Troy. Perhaps your bestial conqueror
laughs as you bleed.
                    Are wild beasts savagely
gnawing you, then leaving your remains
as carrion for Ida's eagle broods?

Ulysses: Don't tell me lies. You cannot hope to fool
Ulysses. I have dealt successfully
with mothers and their schemes; goddesses too.
This is a futile ploy. Where is your son?   570

---

price of victory: see Aulis

72

Andromache: Where's Hector, where are all the Phrygians?
Where's Priam? You're just looking for the one.
I'm seeking everyone and everything.

Ulysses: You'll be forced to declare it if you don't
admit it of your own free will right now.

Andromache: This woman has the power, the need to die,
the wish to die. You cannot do her harm.

Ulysses: Approaching death turns haughty words to screams.

Andromache: You want to bend me with the violence
of fear. So threaten me with life. Death
is what I hope and pray for.

Ulysses: When you've been flogged,
and burned and racked, you'll find that agony
prompts lively disclosure of anything
you try to hide, however unwilling
you are to talk. And that's not all. You'll find
it digs out all your soul's guarded secrets.   580
The need to stop the pain is usually
stronger than ties of family loyalty.

Andromache: So bring your fire, lacerate my flesh,
show your expertise in hideous forms
of torture. Starve me. Drive me mad with thirst.
Try every horror that you can devise.
Thrust shafts of iron up into my guts,
give me a dungeon's pitch-dark, crawling filth,
try anything a conquering hero
attempts when he is angry and afraid.

Ulysses: You are naive to think you can conceal
someone you'll be betraying very soon.

Andromache: I am a mother, and I pride myself
that I will never be controlled by fear.

Ulysses: Don't you see? It is this very love,
and its intensity, that warns the Greeks   590
to think about their own little children.
After a foreign war, after ten years
of fighting, I would feel much less frightened
by those fears that Calchas plays upon
if I had just myself to think about.
But you are nurturing a war my son
Telemachus will someday have to fight.

Andromache: For the life of me, I would not give
Greeks a chance to celebrate. And yet
I must. The pain repressed in me must find
a voice. So gloat, you sons of Atreus,
and you, Ulysses, can, as usual,
cheer them by bringing the good news yourself.
Tell the Greeks that Hector's son is dead.

Ulysses: What proof can you give me that this is true?

Andromache: It is my hope to die both easily
and soon, to be buried beneath the soil   600
of Troy. It is my hope that his ancestral earth
will lie gently upon Hector's ashes.
May I lose all this hope, suffer the worst
my conqueror can do to me unless
what I now tell you is completely true.
My son, lost to the light, lies in a tomb
among the dead. And we have given him
the rites proper to those who've passed away.
He can no longer see the light of day.

Ulysses: Then Fate has been fulfilled, and Hector's line
is now extinct! How happy I will be

74

to bring the Greeks a solid peace at last.
(ULYSSES *begins to leave the stage, then stops. At this point,
as at several others in the play, marked by the notation "inwardly," Seneca gives us a character's thoughts rather than
spoken words. The effect is similar to that of a Shakespearean
aside.*)
What are you doing, Ulysses? The Greeks,
they will believe you, naturally. But *you*,
apparently you're going to believe
someone who should now be obeying you:
the child's mother.

               Still, would any parent
lie in this way? Raw superstition
would surely make her fear that saying this
might somehow turn her lie into the truth.   610

Still, superstition works only when there's
nothing any worse to fear.

                And yet
she swore an oath that makes it credible.
But if it's a false oath—for, after all,
what *could* be worse?

               Come on, my cunning mind,
we need some devious subtlety, some trap:
Try everything your name has come to mean.
The truth will out. She is the child's mother,
watch her carefully.

             There's grief and tears.
She's moaning. Look! She's pacing up and down.
She's tense, straining her ears to pick up sounds.
I do believe she's scared—more scared than sad.
Imagination, that's what's needed now.
(*aloud to* ANDROMACHE)
The decent thing would be to offer you
condolences in your bereavement now,
if you were someone else's mother. But,
poor woman, you I should congratulate
because you've lost your son. He would have died   620

horribly, hurled headlong from that tower
which stands alone among your ruined walls.

Andromache: (*inwardly*)
Life's seeping from my limbs. They shake, give way.
My blood has ceased to flow. It's turned to ice.

Ulysses: (*inwardly*)
She's trembling. There's the chink in her armor:
our mother is betrayed by fear. Well this
should double it.
(*aloud*)   This way, men, this way! Quick!
Get this last blight on Greece, our enemy!
His mother tricked us and hid him away.
He's somewhere here. Root him out, drag him
to me!
(ULYSSES *watches his men search about, but keeps an eye on
Andromache, who pretends not to be looking, but cannot resist
doing so.*)
      Got him? Good work! Come on, bring him,
and hurry up!
(*to* ANDROMACHE) Why do you keep turning   630
and quivering? He *is* dead, isn't he?

Andromache: I wish I had reason to be afraid.
Over the years I have become so used
to terror that my mind is only now
unlearning what it learned so well, so long.

Ulysses: It seems we can't fulfill our holy rite
upon the wall. The infant died too soon,
and can't follow our visionary priest
because fate took him to a better death.
So: we must turn to Calchas' other plan.
He says that we can consecrate the ships
for our return provided we're prepared
to scatter Hector's ashes on the sea,
level his tomb completely to the ground.

So, since the boy escaped his due of death,
it now remains for us to set our hands
to work on Hector's sacred resting place.   640
(ULYSSES *motions his men to start tearing down Hector's
tomb.*)

Andromache: *(inwardly)*
What am I to do now? I'm torn between
two fears, and I don't know which is stronger:
my saintly husband's relics or my son?
God is brutal, and my husband's ghost
is god for me. I swear I love my son
only because it's you, Hector, I see
in him. He must live so I can see
your face again in his.
                    But can I let
them take your ashes from the grave, scatter
your bones upon the devastating sea?
Better my son should die.   650
                    How can you watch
as he is led to an atrocious death?
You are his mother. How can you watch
as they take him along the battlements
and hurl him down?
               I can and will and must
if this will stop his conquerors' abuse
of my dead Hector.
              But the boy would feel
his suffering. Hector's beyond feeling.

Make up your mind! Which are you going to save?

How can you hesitate, how can you be
so thankless? On this side you have Hector—

Oh no, you're wrong! Whichever way you look,
Hector is there. One lives, destined perhaps
to avenge his dead father—
                I cannot   660

77

                              spare both.

                                    Then, of the two, you must preserve
                    the one Greeks fear. That's what you must do.

Ulysses: I'm going to carry out god's will. I shall
                    obliterate this tomb.

Andromache: To think you Greeks
                    sold us his dead body.

Ulysses: I do intend
                    to tear his coffin right out of his tomb.

Andromache: Oh god, please help! Achilles help! Pyrrhus,
                    your father gave my husband's body back.
                    Help us keep it.
Ulysses: In just moments this tomb
                    will lie in pieces all over the plain.

Andromache: You desecrated temples of the gods,
                    even of those who'd favored you. But still,
                    Greeks never tried this sacrilege before.
                    Graves had escaped your passion to destroy.   670
                    But I'll fight back. You're armed and I am not,
                    yet my anger will give me strength. Recall
                    how once the queen of Amazons destroyed
                    whole units of your troops. Think of the Maenad.
                    Bacchus drives her mad, and she then, armed
                    with ivied wand, roams round, controlled by god,
                    not her own mind, striking forests with fear.
                    She wounds, but feels no wounds.
                                              Like them, I'll rush
                    among you and defend that tomb, fighting
                    until I am exhausted, and drop dead—
                    dead as the ashes I am fighting for.

---

his dead body: see Hector

| Ulysses: | (*to his troops who have stopped their demolition of the tomb*) |

Why are you stopping? Are such men as you
moved by a woman's pitiful ravings,
her futile war cry? You had better be
quicker in carrying out what I command.

| Andromache: | Then kill me first, kill me! Oh, all they do | 680 |

is push me back.

     Great Hector, break Death's chains,
and move the earth. For even as a ghost
you're more than match for Ulysses. See here!
He's here! clashing sword on shield, hurling
firebrands. Greeks, do you now see Hector?

Am I the only person to see him?

Ulysses: I'll smash every last stone.

Andromache: (*inwardly*)   Are you insane?
You're wiping out your son and your husband.
Try pleading with the Greeks. That just might work.
It will be instant death for my poor son
when all the masonry falls in. Better
for him to die in any other place
than to be crushed here by his own father,
or for his father's ashes to crumble
beneath his son.
(*prostrating herself before* ULYSSES, *and now speaking aloud*)
     I beg you, Ulysses,   690
upon my knees. Though I've never groveled
at the feet of anyone before,
I'll grovel now. Pity a poor mother.
Be kind and patient. Hear a mother's prayer.

You were exalted, and the powers above
lifted you higher still. Tread more gently
upon the fallen, then. Fortune recalls
some day, when you need it, the kindness shown

79

to those who suffer.
      This I pray for you:
may your wife wait faithfully for you
and may Laertes live to see you home;
your son too, quite a young man now—good luck
to him. May he surpass your hopes, and live   700
longer than his grandfather, and be
wiser than his father.
       Now, in return
I ask just this: pity a poor mother.
Only my child now shares my solitude
and suffering.

Ulysses: Produce your son, then pray.

Andromache: Come out, Astyanax, don't hide:
Your poor mother stole you away.
How sad and pitiful you look.
(ASTYANAX *emerges from the tomb and runs to*
ANDROMACHE.)
Here he is, Ulysses: terror
of a thousand ships. (*to* ASTYANAX) Go
to your master, throw yourself
at his feet and worship him.
When fortune forces you, there's no   710
disgrace. Forget your ancestors
were kings. Forget Priam's empire
was known once throughout the world.
Forget Hector. Play prisoner,
learn how to kneel before your lord.
(ASTYANAX, *sent by* ANDROMACHE's *promptings, goes
over to* ULYSSES *but simply stands in front of him,
perplexed.*)
You can't yet grasp that you must die,
so look at me and imitate:
See how your mother weeps for you.
(*to* ULYSSES)
Another boy-king, years ago,

wept at Troy. And tiny Priam's
tears softened the fierce intent
of Hercules—so vastly strong   720
all wild beasts fled at his approach.
That hero smashed on through Death's gates,
he opened up the pathway back
from darkness below.

                          Conquered
by tears of his tiny foe,
"Be king!" he said, "Sit high upon
your father's throne and rule the land,
but act in better faith." That's what
it meant to be conquered by him.
Be moderate in anger, as
was Hercules. Or do you just   730
admire his strength? Before your feet
there lies a suppliant who is
no smaller than the suppliant
Priam, begging for his life.
Fortune can take the crown of Troy
Wherever it likes.

Ulysses: This mother's grief and shock really move me.
But still it moves me even more to think
of Greek mothers. For if this boy grows up
they will have very good reason for grief.

Andromache: You think he can stir new life in a town
reduced to ashes? Look around! You think
these hands will rebuild Troy? If this is Troy's   740
one hope, she has no hope; we Trojans are
so dead we could not possibly give cause
for fear to anyone.

                    Surely you don't
think that his father will inspire him now:
that corpse, dragged in the dust?

---

your father's throne: see Laomedon

And once Troy fell,
even his father's courage would have snapped:
total disaster breaks men totally.

Still, if he really must be penalized,
make him a household slave, and make him bend
his royal head in the most terrible
humiliation that one can inflict.
Who would deny this privilege to a king?

Ulysses: Calchas, not Ulysses, rejects your plea.

Andromache: You're an artist in treachery and crime.   750
But, as for manliness, you've never once
come out victorious in a fair fight.
The cunning trickery of your evil mind
has killed Greeks, not just Trojans. So don't blame
a priest, don't blame the gods. They are guiltless.
You planned this crime yourself.
You used to do
your soldiering at night, but now, you've found
the guts to strike alone during the day.
How brave you are at murdering a child!

Ulysses: The Greeks know well enough that I'm a man.
Trojans know it too well. I don't have time
to waste the day in stupid arguments.
The fleet is starting to weigh anchor now.

Andromache: Just grant a short delay: be generous.   760
I'll then obey both you and my duty
as parent to her dying son. Sorrow
is greedy. Let me satisfy it with
a last embrace.

Ulysses: I only wish I could

---

soldiering at night: see Diomedes

take pity on you. Time, a short delay,
is all that I can give, and I'll give that.
Cry as you will with all the tears you wish.
Weeping makes sadness easier to bear.

Andromache: Dear child, proof of my love, you gave luster
to our ruined home and land. You are
Troy's last death, the Greeks' last fear, your mother's
futile hope. I was mad when I prayed
you'd win honor in war, like your father,
and that you'd live as long as grandfather.
God ignored my prayers. You'll never be   770
lord and master in Troy's palace walls,
lawmaker for your people, conqueror
of foreign nations, leading them beneath
your yoke. You'll never rout and slaughter Greeks,
drag Pyrrhus in the dust. Your tender hand
will never bear a boy's tiny weapons,
you'll not scatter wild game, hunting it far
and wide in dense forest, showing how bold
you are. You will not live to be a youth,
to lead the horsemen when we celebrate
the Games of Troy, or leap nimbly among
the altars when the echoing trumpets set   780
quick rhythms for the ancient rituals
in shrines Greeks call barbaric.

                            You will die
more grimly than in combat. Now our walls
will see a sight to stir more tears of grief
than when great Hector died.

Ulysses:
                                  Turn off the tears,
obedient mother. Your great pain does not
have any sense of when it ought to stop.

Andromache: Ulysses, the delay I ask is short:

---

the Games of Troy: a particularly *Roman* festival activity for young boys

just time to cry. Grant me the right to use
my hand to close his eyes although he's still
alive.
(*to* ASTYANAX) You have to die. You are so small
but, even now, they are afraid of you.
Your country waits. Buoyed with freedom's pride,   790
go, join the other Trojans who are free.

(ASTYANAX *breaks from* ULYSSES *and clings to* ANDROMA-
CHE'*s skirts.*)

Astyanax: Pity me, mother.

Andromache: It is no use
snuggling to me, holding your mother's hand.
I can't do anything to help you now.

You huddle to your mother like a calf
who's frightened when he hears the lion's roar.
Fiercely, the lion pushes the mother
aside; for his prey is the little one.
He snaps the tiny spine with those vast jaws,
and then hauls him away.
                       That's how your foe
will tear you from my side.
                   Take my kisses,
my tears, the hair I've torn from my head,
and run to meet your father loaded with   800
these gifts from me. Tell him just this. Tell him
mother is angry, say to him: "If ghosts
remain concerned for those they loved in life,
if passion is remembered once the fires
have left us ashes, Hector, will you go
much farther in your cruel neglect? Is your
Andromache to serve a Greek man's will?
Will you just lie there, idle and passive?
Achilles—he came back."
                  Again I give
my hair, I give my tears—all I have left

after my grief for Hector's death. Please give
this kiss to your father.
(ANDROMACHE *takes away* ASTYANAX's *cloak*)
Leave your mother
this cloak to comfort her. My sepulcher
and its dear ghost have touched it. So my lips   810
must search it. For perhaps there is some trace
of Hector's ashes here.

Ulysses: She clearly won't
stop crying, men. So get this obstacle
to the Greek fleet out of here. Be quick!

(ULYSSES *and his* SOLDIERS *tear* ASTYANAX *away from*
ANDROMACHE *and march him away.* ANDROMACHE *col-
lapses, sobbing, and is comforted by* HECUBA, *who now enters with the* CHORUS.)

Chorus: Where are we doomed to live, we prisoners?—
Where?—
Thessaly's mountains, shadowed vale of Tempe—
Phthia, breeding ground of fighting men,
Achilles' home—
Trachis, ruggedly rich in horses grazing—
Iolcos, vast sea's mistress—
Crete, sprawling hundred-citied—   820
Tiny Gyrton, barren Tricce—
Mothone, sparkling with myriad streams,
shadowed by Oeta's woods,
last resting place of Hercules
whose mighty bow twice
leveled Troy to dust—

Or could it be—
Olenus, sparsely peopled—
Pleuron, hated by the goddess of the hunt—

---

goddess of the hunt: Diana

Troezen, curving out into the sea—
Proud Prothoüs' realm of Pelion,
a mountain that
giants once piled high on Ossa
in an attempt to overthrow the gods?—
There is a hollow in that mountain,   830
eaten away by time;
and it was there that once a boy,
a savage boy, was taught
melodies upon the lute,
and primed to lust for battle
by the songs of war
his tutor Chiron made him learn—
Achilles—

Perhaps it will be—
Carystos, veined with marble—
Calchis on the shores of the restless sea,
swept by the surging channel tides—
Calydnae, islands any breeze can blow you to—
Gonoessa, always windy—   840
Enispe, chilled by northern gales—
Peparethos, off the coast of Attica—
Eleusis, holy city of the mysteries—
Salamis, home of Ajax—
Calydon, where the wild boar lived—
Thessaly, washed by the slow waters of Titaressos
flowing down beneath the sea to Hell—

Perhaps—
Bessa—Scarphe—Pylos, an old man's kingdom—
Pharis—Pisa, loved by Jupiter—
Elis, home of the Olympic games—   850
Little do we care where the storm winds blow us!
Send us to any land—
except Sparta, Helen's city,
which savaged Troy and Greece—
except Argos and Mycenae,

home of Agamemnon and his ancestors—
except, above all, except
tiny Neritos—
tinier Zacynthos—
and Ithaca
darkening seas with treacherous reefs,
home of Ulysses—

What fate awaits you, Hecuba?
Who will be your master,
taking you home to show his people?—
Whose kingdom will you die in?—   860

ACT IV

Enter HELEN, *escorted by* FEMALE ATTENDANTS. *The*
TROJAN WOMEN *do not notice her, but cluster around* HE-
CUBA *and* ANDROMACHE.

Helen: (*inwardly*)
If your marriage brings unhappiness,
sorrow and heartbreak, anguish, blood, and death,
then Helen should have given you blessing.
Troy has been conquered; but I am still forced
to harm the Trojans. I have been ordered
to deceive them, say Polyxena
is going to marry Pyrrhus; and I must
dress her in Greek clothes and jewelry.
She is Paris' sister, doomed to be
snared by my skill, destroyed by my deceit.
Well, let her be deceived. Indeed I think
it will be easier for her that way.
To die when you don't know you're going to die,
that's everybody's prayer, then there's no fear.

I hesitate.
          But why? If you're compelled
to do a crime, responsibility
rests with the person who compels the act.   870
(*aloud to* POLYXENA)
Noble girl of Dardanus' house,
god starts to smile on you and your city
after your great sorrows, granting you
a marriage bed teeming with fruitful life,
a wedding neither Priam nor his Troy,
if they survived, would ever dower you with.
The greatest name in Greece for whom the plains

88

of Thessaly spread out a wide kingdom
wants you to be his lawful wife, to join
in holy sacrament with him. The great
Tethys, and many other sea spirits
will call you their own, and, above all,
Thetis, who calms swelling waves with power
serene. The instant Pyrrhus takes your hand,   880
Achilles' father and his grandfather
will have in you the daughter-in-law they want.
Take off your filthy funeral garb. Put on
this festive dress. Forget captivity.
We'll have an expert comb and set your hair.
Perhaps your sufferings will bring you to
a greater kingdom than the one you had.
Many do well in captivity.

Andromache: The final touch for Trojans in their hour
of doom was missing until now!
                        A feast
to celebrate. Troy's wreckage burns all round.
What glorious timing for a wedding day!
Who'd dare deny it? Who'd be hesitant   890
to share a bed that Helen recommends?
Two nations you have shattered, ruined, smashed.
See these graves of mighty men, those bones
unburied, bleached, scattered across the plains,
the withered petals of your bride's bouquet.
Asia's blood and Europe's flowed for you.
And you took pleasure as you watched the fight,
wondering which side to pray for.
                      Go on, prepare
your wedding. There's no need for marriage torch
or ceremonial fire. Troy is aglow
with light enough for this new wedding day.   900
Celebrate Pyrrhus' marriage, women
of Troy. Celebrate it with the fire
of passion it deserves: drumming your hands
against your breasts with groans and cries of grief.

Helen: People overcome with bitterness
and sorrow tend to be illogical,
obstinate—sometimes they even hate
others who are their fellow sufferers.
Though you are ready to convict me now
without fair trial, I can make a case
in my defense. For I have suffered more
than you.

              Yes you, Andromache, can weep
for Hector, Hecuba for Priam. But
when I weep for Paris I must weep
alone and silently.

                You think it's harsh,
it's grim, it's odious to be a slave?
Well I have borne the yoke that you now bear.   910
For ten years I've been a slave.

            So Troy
has been destroyed, your homes and culture trampled
in the dirt? To lose your homeland's hard.
But it is harder still when you're afraid
of going back.

           You still have company
to lighten your afflictions, whereas I
am target for the spite of both conquered
and conqueror. You don't yet know which Greek
is going to drag you off to be his whore.
For long it hung uncertain, wavering,
pending the outcome of the lottery.
No benefit of a lottery for me.
My master just hauled me off.

             Am I
to blame for all these wars, and for Troy's fall?
I am, true, if it was a Spartan ship
that cut across your seas. But it was not.
Trojan sailors took me as plunder,   920
the bride of Venus the Victorious
rewarding Paris' judgment.

            Please forgive

this item of plunder. I'll soon be called
to make my plea before an angry judge.
Menelaus' judgment now remains.

Stop crying over your own broken heart
Andromache. Spare just a tear for her—
(*indicating* POLYXENA)
I can hardly restrain myself from tears.

Andromache: Poor girl! How horrible her fate must be
if Helen weeps for her.
                          Helen—why would
she cry?
               What crime is Ulysses hatching?
Where will they throw her from? From Ida's peaks,
or from the steepest rock in the city?
Perhaps they will take her to Sigeum,
high on the cliffs, and looking down upon
its shallow bay. Into the sea's vastness
they will hurl her.
                    Out with it! Tell us,   930
you two-faced traitor, what you keep from us.
Any fate would sit more easily
than having Pyrrhus in our family,
as Hecuba's and Priam's son-in-law.
Tell us the punishment you plan for us.
Spare us at least the misery of deceit.
We're all ready to die as you can see.

Helen: (*to* POLYXENA)
I wish Calchas had also ordered me
killed by the sword. Then I would not be forced
to linger in the light I hate to see.
Would I could die there on Achilles' tomb,
beside you, butchered by the mad Pyrrhus.   940

Achilles wants you, poor Polyxena,
he wants you brought and given to him, he wants

you slaughtered on his ashes so that he
can be your husband in Elysium.

Andromache: *(inwardly)*
See how a great, courageous soul is glad
to hear sentence of death. She's reaching for
the ceremonial glow of royal clothes,
she lets them comb her hair.

                        For to marry
Pyrrhus—that, she reckoned, was true death.
This death she reckons is a true wedding.

But her mother, already torn with grief
at what she's heard, has slipped. She's going to faint!
(ANDROMACHE *runs to* HECUBA*'s side and speaks aloud.*)
Get up, poor woman, up! Don't lose courage,   950
don't let go!
(inwardly again) She is, life is, so frail;
it hangs on such a slender thread. It would
take little now to make her whole again.
(aloud)
She's breathing, coming back to life!
(inwardly)
                           When death
meets pain for the first time, he runs away.

Hecuba: So Achilles, then, is still alive,
still fighting back, punishing Troy. Paris,
you should have struck a harder blow! Even
his ashes and his tomb thirst for our blood.

Not long ago, I teemed with life. I had
a flock of children all clinging to me,
I was exhausted mothering each one,
sharing my kisses and my love around.
I have only her to pray for now,   960
to keep me company, lighten sorrow,
and help me rest. She is Hecuba's brood,

the only voice that still calls me mother.
Oh harsh and barren life, please slip away!
Grant me just one child's death that I don't have
to watch. My cheeks are wet. My tears well up
and fall like rain. I am defeated now.

Andromache: Hecuba, you should cry for us, for us.
Who knows where we'll be scattered when the fleet
Sets sail? But home's dear earth will blanket her.   970

Helen: You'll envy her still more when you have learned
the lot awaiting you.

Andromache: There's some detail
of my torment that I've not heard about?

Helen: The lottery's complete. It has assigned
masters to each captive woman here.

Andromache: Whose bed- and chambermaid am I to be?
Tell me which one I have to call master?

Helen: Your name was drawn first. Pyrrhus got you.

Andromache: Cassandra! Your madness has benefits,
it seems. As Phoebus' priestess you are spared
the lottery.

Helen: The greatest king of kings,
takes her.

Hecuba: Be glad, rejoice, Polyxena!
What would Cassandra give for your wedding?
What would Andromache? Does anyone
want to call Hecuba his very own?

---

king of kings: Agamemnon

93

Helen: He didn't want you since there's not much life
          in you. You go as prize to Ulysses.   980

Hecuba: What makes anyone so powerful,
          so bestial and ruthless that he can
          arrange a lottery that raffles off
          kings to kings in blatant injustice?
          What sick-minded god allots captives
          like this? How cruel a judge, how merciless
          to suffering! He has no sense at all
          of who should be whose master. He metes out
          destinies unjust to the helpless.
          Achilles' weapons killed Hector, my son.
          Ulysses first won the weapons, then
          won me. I am truly a prisoner,
          walled in completely by disaster now.
          I admit defeat. I'm not ashamed
          to be a slave. I am ashamed *he* is   990
          my master.
                        This man plundered Achilles.
          Is he to take all that was Hector's too?
          Never will his barren land, shut in
          by raging seas contain my grave, I swear.
          Lead on, Ulysses, lead the way, I won't
          hang back. I'll follow my master. But then
          my luck will follow me. There'll be no calm
          upon the seas. Wind and wave will lash
          and savage you. War, fire, and each horror
          Priam and I endured will turn on you
          in all their fury. But, in the meantime,
          you have a foretaste of your punishment.
          I used up your lot. I took away
          your chance of a real prize.
          (*Enter* PYRRHUS *with an* ARMED ESCORT. *He heads di-*
          rectly for POLYXENA, *passing* HECUBA, *who taunts him.*)
                                    Pyrrhus himself.
          He's in a hurry and his face is grim.
          What stops you, Pyrrhus? Why not kill me too?   1000

Then both Achilles' in-laws will be dead.
Killing old people is your specialty,
Come on, don't lose the honor of my blood.
(PYRRHUS *and the* SOLDIERS *escort* POLYXENA *away.*
There is no resistance. The TROJAN WOMEN *watch*
passively.)
Go, take her, desecrate the gods above
with human sacrifice and desecrate
the dead. What curse will I call down on you?
I wish on you the voyage you deserve
for rituals like this. So may the curse
that I will call on to destroy the ship
that carries me destroy the whole Greek fleet,
every last one of all your thousand ships.
(HECUBA *and* ANDROMACHE *retire upstage. The* CHORUS
moves down.)

Chorus: It's sweet to see your whole nation
suffering as you suffer—
moaning as you moan—   1010
Grief and tears bite
much less savagely
when everyone is weeping—
You always, always wish evil on others
when sorrow strikes—
You love to see thousands go to their doom—
It's comforting to know you're not alone,
you've not been singled out
to bear the anguish and the pain—
No one ever refuses to suffer
what everyone else must suffer—

Obliterate the happy—
then no one will think himself unhappy
however unhappy he may be—
Wipe out the wealthy and their gold—
wipe out the men with acres of rich land
to plow with fifty teams—   1020

95

then the world's poor
will rise up from their knees
with dignity restored—

There is no misery without comparison—

It is so sweet,
to stand amid total ruin,
and see nobody smiling—
But when yours is the only ship that sinks
as you cross the sea—
when you swim ashore naked,
and alone—
then you cry, then you lament your fate—
Storms and shipwreck seem
not so unseasonable
when a thousand other vessels sink   1030
before your eyes—
as you cling to your plank,
drifting landward,
while gales lash waves
and others
cannot make it—

When the sheep with shimmering golden fleece
carried Phrixus and Helle
across the sea,
Phrixus mourned when Helle drowned,
lost in the middle of the waves—

But when the Flood came—
When Pyrrha and Deucalion
looked out and saw the sea—
saw nothing but the sea—   1040
and knew themselves the last survivors
of the human race—
they did not weep—

Now we can cry together and have company in tears—
but soon trumpet call
summons sailor to ship—
and sails and oars' sweep
speed the fleet on its way—
scattering cries—
isolating sorrows—
as we surge across the deep—
as the shoreline retreats—
as sea looms large and land shrinks,
as the summit of Ida sinks
below the horizon—
What will we feel?

Son and mother, mother and son   1050
will point to where Troy glows—
They will say as they point their fingers
from afar—
"Do you see where smoke
snakes high into the air?
Do you see where clouds are black?
There, that's Troy"—

And that's the way the Trojans will recognize their
    home.

ACT V

Enter TALTHYBIUS.

Talthybius: How harsh fate is! How vicious, pitiful!
How ugly! The ten years of war have seen
no atrocity to rival this.
(*looking to* ANDROMACHE)
Should I tell you of your bereavement first?
Perhaps, old woman, (*indicating* HECUBA) I should tell
    you yours.

Hecuba: No matter whose bereavement makes you weep,
You weep for mine. The others have to bear   1060
losses that are individual.
But each disaster crushes me because
everything that's lost was mine to lose.
God help anyone who's Hecuba's.

Talthybius: The girl was sacrificed, the boy was thrown
down from the battlements. But each met death
with great nobility and fortitude.

Andromache: The whole story: tell us, step by step,
about this double crime, this double sin.
When grief is total, there's a strange pleasure
in hearing each detail of agony.
So go ahead and tell us everything.

Talthybius: One tower still stands above your ruined Troy.
Priam would often go there, sit on top,
direct the fighting from the battlements.
The old man sat his grandson tenderly

98

upon his knee, and from that vantage point   1070
showed him his father's exploits in those days
when Hector routed Greeks, pursuing them
with fire and sword as they ran off in fear.
This tower, which used to be a famous, fine
segment of the city walls, today
was just a grisly precipice, circled
with crowds of officers and men. Leaving
the ships, the crews crushed shank to shank. Some found
a distant hill with unobstructed view.
Some climbed a tall cliff, and stood at the top   1080
on tiptoe. Beeches, pines, and bays became
observation points. The whole forest
shuddered with people hanging down like fruit.
One man sought out a sheared-off mountain face;
others made half-burned homes their seats, on stones
jutting from ruined walls. One spectator
brutishly and sacrilegiously
sat on Hector's tomb.

                       Then, through the crowds
and through the desolation, Ulysses
strode, proudly dragging Priam's small grandson.
Unhesitatingly, the boy mounted   1090
the walls, and when he reached the tower-top,
he stood still, fiercely surveyed the crowd,
glowing with courage like a wild beast's cub,
tender and small, perhaps not strong enough,
as yet, to savage with his fangs, but still
growling with menace, making as if to bite,
pulsing with noble rage. Though tightly gripped
by his enemy's good hand, the boy
showed mettle and pride, moving the men,
the officers, and even Ulysses
to tears. Everyone wept, except the boy
that they were weeping for.

                        As Ulysses
began the dedication, prayed the prayers
Calchas told him to pray, and as he called   1100

the cruel gods to grace this sacrifice
with their presence, the boy himself leaped down
into the heart of Priam's realm.

Andromache: No witch,
no Scythian nomad, no remote tribesman,
ignorant of justice and of right,
would act like this! Proverbially cruel
Busiris was, yet he did not butcher
children on his altars. Diomedes
did not serve children's limbs to his horses,
though they ate flesh.
                              Who will pick up your limbs
and bury them, Astyanax?

Talthybius: What limbs   1110
are to be found after a fall like that?
His bones were crushed and scattered by the drop.
When his weight hit the ground so far below,
his face, his body, all that so recalled
Hector was pulped. His neck broke when it hit
a rock; his skull cracked open, and his brains
poured out. Nothing remains that would suggest
a body.

Andromache: Then he's still like his father.

Talthybius: The boy had fallen from high on the walls.
The Greeks first wept for the atrocity
they'd done, en masse. And then those same people
came back for yet another criminal act,   1120
this time at Achilles' grave.
                              The straits
of Rhoeteum lash the far side of the tomb
caressingly. But, on the other side,
it is encompassed by a plain, rising
gently at the edges to create
a valley in between—the shape suggests

a theater, in fact.
                    The crowd rushed in,
filling each open space. Some of them think
this death will solve the problem, end delays,
and launch the ships. And some rejoice to see
the foe's last limb trimmed back. But many in
this fickle mob hate the atrocity
they see yet cannot tear their eyes away.
Crowds of Trojans too, trembling with fear,   1130
came to witness this final chapter
of the fall of Troy.
                    Now, suddenly,
the whole procession is in view: rows
of flaming torches, such as you would see
at a real wedding. Helen was there
as maid of honor, though her head was bowed
in grief. "Vile Helen," every Trojan prayed,
"We hope to god that your Hermione
will be married like this, and that you too
will soon rejoin your husband—on his grave!"
Trojans and Greeks alike were terrified
and stunned. In modesty Polyxena
lowered her eyes; her face was radiant.
Her beauty's sunset shone more gloriously
than did its brightest day, just as Phoebus
likes to keep us in fascinated daze
with softer luminescence as he sets,   1140
and stars return to gleam and daylight fades
shimmering to dark at night's approach.
The crowd, like most crowds, is intrigued and gawks,
readiest as ever to applaud
a thing that's going to die.
                         Her beauty stirs
some onlookers; her tender youth beguiles
others. Then there are those who brood upon
the unpredictability of life.
Sheer courage in the face of death moves men.

She walks ahead of Pyrrhus. They admire,
they all pity her. Thoughts race, hearts pound.
As she attained the mountaintop—it seemed
so steep—the young man stopped and took his stand
high on his father's grave.

Heroically,   1150

she turned to face the blow, did not retreat
one step. And from her eyes defiance, pride
beamed fierce. Her courage struck both awe and fear
in every heart. Pyrrhus was slow to kill—
which was itself a novel prodigy.
He drew his sword then thrust the steel hilt-deep
in her. Blood spurted from beneath the gash
the death wound, as it penetrated, made.
Nor did her spirit fail her as she died.
She threw herself upon the ground, face first,
as if attacking it in wrath to make
the earth lie heavy on Achilles' bones.

Those who had come together wept: Trojans   1160
gave muffled, timid moans; their conquerors
cried aloud, more ostentatiously.
The holy ritual had been performed.
And yet the blood spilled did not flow in streams
upon the surface of the ground. The grave
savagely sucked it in and drank it down.

Hecuba: Sail, Greek heroes, sail, sail safely home!
Spread all your canvas, and the winds can blow
your fleet across the seas you've longed to cross!
You're quite safe now. The boy and girl are dead.
The war is over.

Where can I go to cry,

to spit out what it is that stands between
this old woman and death?

Should I weep for

my daughter, grandson, husband—my country,
for everything, or for myself alone?

102

Death is my only prayer.
Oh death, you come   1170
so violently to babies and young girls,
so mercilessly everywhere you go.
I am the only one you fear and shun
and force to live.
Last night Troy fell. Nightlong
I hunted you in flame and fight, but you
eluded my yearning embrace. Fires raged,
foes killed, houses fell. Nothing touched me.
I was so near to Priam, yet so far away.

Talthybius: Prisoners, hurry to the sea! The ships
are hoisting sail. The fleet is moving out.

Exeunt omnes.

Glossary

The brief summaries given here are based on the Senecan versions of the myths. Other ancient writers often give different accounts. Variants are mentioned only where necessary for clarity. An asterisk next to a name indicates that it has its own entry elsewhere in the glossary. The Latin names are used except when an accepted English version exists.

Absyrtus Son of Aeetes* and brother of Medea;* killed by Medea, who then threw his limbs into the sea as she fled from Colchis.*

Acastus King of Iolcus,* in Thessaly;* son of Pelias,* Jason's* uncle and enemy.

Achaean Greek.

Acharnia An area in Attica* north of Athens.

Acheron One of four frequently mentioned rivers of the Greek underworld.

Achilles Son of the goddess Thetis* and her mortal husband, Peleus,* born in Phthia* in Thessaly;* educated by the centaur Chiron.* At the outbreak of the Trojan War, Thetis disguised him as a girl (to keep him from being drafted into the army) and kept him on the island of Scyros,* where he raped a girl named Deidamia, thus fathering Pyrrhus.* Eventually he betrayed himself to the Greek military recruiters, led by Ulysses,* by his fascination with the weapons they brought.

Acte Another name for Attica.*

Admetus Mythical king of Thessaly* whose wife, Alcestis,* died in his place but was brought back from the dead by Hercules.*

Aeacus Father of Peleus;* grandfather of Achilles;* frequently thought of as a ruler among the dead.

Aeetes King of Colchis;* father of Medea* and Absyrtus.*

Aegaleus A mountain range in Attica.*

Aegeus   Father of Theseus.★ The Aegean Sea was named for him. See Sunion.

Aeolus   Father of Sisyphus;★ ancestor of Creon★ of Corinth★ and his daughter Creusa.★

Aeson   Father of Jason;★ king of Iolcus,★ deposed by Pelias.★

Aetna   A volcano in Sicily; mythical abode of Vulcan,★ god of fire.

Agamemnon   King of Mycenae;★ son of Atreus,★ brother of Menelaus.★ Leader of the Greek expedition against Troy,★ he sacrificed his own daughter to obtain favorable winds (see Aulis). His quarrel with Achilles,★ who objected to Agamemnon's seizure of his concubine Briseis,★ is a major motif of Homer's *Iliad*.

Ajax   (1) The "Greater" Ajax, son of Telamon, was the best of the Greek warriors at Troy★ after Achilles;★ he committed suicide when the dead Achilles' armor was awarded to Ulysses★ rather than to him. (2) The "Lesser" Ajax, son of Oileus,★ was shipwrecked on his return from the Trojan War.

Alcestis   Wife of Admetus.★ She was brought back to life by Hercules★ after she died in her husband's place.

Alcides   A descendant of Alc(a)eus, the father of Amphitryon; always = Hercules★ in Seneca.

Alcmena   Wife of Amphitryon. Seduced by Jupiter,★ who disguised himself as her husband, she gave birth to Hercules.★

Alpheus   A river in the Peloponnesus.

Althaea   Mother of Meleager,★ whose life, she was told at his birth, could last only as long as a certain log burning in the fire. She immediately seized the log from the flames, but years later, when Meleager killed her beloved brothers, in anger she threw it back into a fire. As predicted, Meleager died when the log was consumed.

Amazons   A group of nomadic, man-hating female warriors whose homeland is usually given as the region around the Black Sea: Maeotis,★ Thermodon,★ Pontus.★ The Greeks had several mythical battles with them. Theseus★ fought them and forced Antiope★ to become his wife; she bore him a son, Hippolytus,★ but Theseus later put her to death. Penthesilea★ led a band of Amazons against the Greeks at Troy and was killed by Achilles.★

Amor   Cupid;★ especially popular among the Roman poets because his name spelled backward is Roma. In Vergil's *Aeneid* and elsewhere in Latin literature, Aeneas, founder of the Roman race, is Amor's brother.

Amyclae   A city near Sparta;★ Sparta's "twin city." Its name is often used to indicate Sparta itself.

Ancaeus   An Argonaut from Tegea, in the Peloponnesus, who replaced Tiphys★ as helmsman of the *Argo*★ after Tiphys' death.

Andromache   Daughter of Eetion;★ wife of Hector;★ mother of Astyanax.★

She was taken from Troy★ by Pyrrhus★ after the city's fall and was ultimately married to Hector's brother, Helenus.★

Antenor   A Trojan warrior; husband of Theano, priestess of the goddess Minerva (Pallas)★ at Troy.★ In some traditions Antenor and Aeneas, son of Venus,★ betrayed Troy to the Greeks.

Antiope   A queen of the Amazons.★ She appears in three distinct traditions: (1) as a wife of Theseus★ (see Amazons); (2) as the queen whose girdle Hercules★ must win as his ninth labor; (3) as mother of Amphion and Zethus, the builders of Thebes'★ walls.

Aonia   Thebes.★

Aphidnae   An area of Attica★ near Marathon.★

Apollo   See Phoebus.

Aquilo   See Boreas.

Araxes   An Armenian river, today the Aras; often a symbol to Roman writers of the eastern boundary of Roman power.

Arcadia   A mountainous and primitive part of Greece whose inhabitants were supposedly the earliest inhabitants of Greece; they are often depicted as people of either ideal simplicity or primitive barbarism. Roman tradition maintained that the first settlement of the site of Rome was made by an exiled king of Arcadia, Evander, a descendant of Lycaon,★ "Wolfman."

Arctus   The constellation Ursa Major (the Great Bear or Big Dipper), the main constellation used by the Greeks for navigation. The Phoenicians and Carthaginians sailed by the Lesser Bear (Ursa Minor), known as Cynosura. In myth the Great Bear is Callisto,★ daughter of Lycaon.★ After her rape by Jupiter★ she was turned into a bear by Diana,★ then saved from hunters by Jupiter,★ who placed her in the skies.

Argo   The ship that conveyed Jason★ and the Argonauts (i.e., "sailors in *Argo*") to and from Colchis;★ in some traditions, the first ship ever made. *Argo*'s keel was made of oak from the prophetic shrine of Dodona; the vessel itself could speak.

Argos   A major city in the Peloponnesus, often not distinguished from Mycenae.★ The adjective "Argive" is often used to mean "Greek."

Ariadne   Daughter of Minos,★ king of Crete, and of Pasiphae,★ his wife; sister of Phaedra★ and the Minotaur.★ She fell in love with Theseus★ and saved him from death in the labyrinth by supplying him with a thread made by Daedalus★ which enabled Theseus to escape from the labyrinth after killing the Minotaur, who was imprisoned there. Theseus took Ariadne with him as he left Crete but abandoned her on the island of Naxos. She was saved by Bacchus,★ who made her his wife and ultimately set her in the heavens as a star.

Assaracus   Great-grandson of Dardanus;★ brother of Jupiter's★ Trojan lover Ganymede; great-grandfather of Aeneas, who was regarded by some Roman writers as founder of the Roman people.

Assyria   Very roughly the equivalent of parts of modern Iraq; to Roman
       writers it included Syria as well. The area was proverbial for its
       luxurious living and particularly for its perfumes.
Astyanax   Son of Hector* and Andromache;* killed on instructions from
       Calchas.*
Athos   A high peninsula jutting out into the Aegean from the Thracian
       coast.
Atreus   Father of Agamemnon* and Menelaus* (who are collectively
       known as the Atridae); feuded with his brother Thyestes,* whose
       children he murdered and served as a meal to their father.
Attica   The section of Greece in which the city of Athens is situated.
Aulis   A coastal city of Euboea, in Greece, from which the Greeks sailed
       to Troy.* Here, to obtain favorable winds, Agamemnon* sacrificed
       his daughter Iphigenia at the bidding of the priest Calchas.*
Ausonian   A general poetic term for the non-Greek-speaking ancient in-
       habitants of Italy.
Auster   The south wind, bringer of clouds and rain.
Avernus   The Italian equivalent of Taenarum;* a lake near Cumae, in the
       Bay of Naples area, which supposedly welled up from the
       underworld.
Bacchus   God of wine, proverbially beautiful; also known as Lyaeus, Liber,
       Bromius, and Dionysus.
Baetis   The river Guadalquivir, in Spain.
Bessa   A small town near Scarphe,* in Locris (central Greece).
Boötes   A constellation near the Greater and Lesser Bears.
Boreas   The north wind, father of Calais* and Zetes.*
Briseis   A woman from Lyrnesos* captured by Achilles* and kept as his
       lover. She was seized from Achilles by Agamemnon* when Aga-
       memnon was forced to relinquish his own captive lover, Chryseis.*
Bromius   See Bacchus.
Busiris   A mythical Egyptian king who sacrificed at the altar of Jupiter* all
       foreigners who entered his land.
Calais   Son of Boreas;* twin of Zetes; drove off the Harpies* from their
       homeland; killed (with Zetes) by Hercules.*
Calchas   A Greek prophet who told Agamemnon* he must sacrifice his
       own daughter to obtain favorable winds for the voyage to Troy.*
       He also ordered that Astyanax* and Polyxena* be sacrificed to
       secure the Greeks' safe return.
Callisto   Daughter of Lycaon.* See Arctus.
Calydnae   Two small islands off the coast of Asia Minor, near Troy.*
Calydon   Town in Aetolia (Greece), most famous in myth for a boar hunt
       which took place there. It was during this hunt that Meleager*
       killed his uncles.
Camena   The Latin equivalent of the Greek *Mousa*, Muse. Seneca's choice

of this word to indicate the mother of the Greek bard Orpheus★ is striking, as Roman poets tended to use *Musa* rather than *Camena* in reference to Greek poetic muses. Compare his use of the Latin term *fescennine*.★

Carystos   A city at the south end of the island of Euboea (Greece).

Cassandra   Daughter of Priam★ and Hecuba;★ priestess of Phoebus.★ She agreed to become the god's lover in return for the gift of prophecy but finally refused to have sex with him. Phoebus punished her by decreeing that no one would believe her prophecies. After the fall of Troy★ she was assigned to Agamemnon★ as his prize.

Castor   Brother of Pollux;★ one of *Argo*'s crew. The two brothers, who spent half of each year alive and half dead, were known and worshiped together as the divine Dioscuri ("Boys of Zeus," in Greek) and were believed to protect sailors. Castor was famous for his horsemansip and his horse Cyllarus; Pollux was famous for his boxing.

Caucasus   A mountain or mountainous area near the Caspian Sea; the mythical site where Prometheus★ was kept in chains.

Caycus   The principal river of Mysia★ (Turkey).

Cecrops   A mythical forebear of the Athenian people, half man, half snake. The adjective "Cecropian" is often used as a general equivalent of "Athenian."

Cephallenia   An Ionian★ island southwest of Ithaca; the name is often used to indicate Ithaca.

Cerberus   A mythical three-headed dog who guarded the entrance/exit of the underworld.

Ceres   Mother Earth; goddess of crops.

Chalcis   A powerful city of Euboea (Greece), one of whose colonies was Cumae, in Italy.

Charybdis   A dangerous mythical whirlpool in the sea, facing Scylla.★

Chimaera   A mythical monster, part goat, part lion, part snake.

Chiron   A centaur (half horse, half man) associated with Mount Pelion,★ in Thessaly;★ tutor of Achilles.★ Although immortal, he was wounded by Hercules★ with a poisoned arrow, and in his pain begged to be allowed to die.

Chryse   A small town near Troy.★

Chryseis   Daughter of Chryses, a priest of Phoebus;★ taken as a concubine by Agamemnon★ but released when Phoebus sent a plague upon the Greek army. Agamemnon took Briseis★ from Achilles★ as a replacement for Chryseis.

Cicero   A Roman orator of the first century B.C. In his first oration against Catiline (a Roman noble who Cicero believed was plotting to overthrow the government), Cicero appealed to Catiline to "free the citizens from fear" by leaving Rome. Seneca's Creon★ echoes these words in *Medea*.

Glossary

Cilla   A small town near Chryse.*

Cnossos   The principal city of ancient Crete; home of Minos,* Phaedra,* and the Minotaur.

Colchis   Medea's* hometown, on the eastern shore of the Black Sea (now in the Soviet Union).

Corinth   A city on the isthmus connecting the Peloponnesus to northern Greece.

Corus   The northwest wind.

Cossack   = Scythian* in these translations.

Creon   King of Corinth;* father of Creusa.*

Creusa   Daughter of Creon.*

Cupid   God of love = Amor,* often represented by Romans as the son of Venus.*

Cybele   The earth-mother goddess (also known as Cybebe), whose cult was centered on Mount Ida,* near Troy,* Her cult was also well established in Rome.

Cyclades   Islands in the Aegean.

Cygnus   The invulnerable son of Neptune,* whom Achilles* killed by strangulation; Neptune metamorphosed him into a swan.

Cyllarus   The special horse of Castor.*

Daedalus   An Athenian craftsman, who helped the Cretan queen Pasiphae* consummate her love for a white bull by making her a cowsuit of wood. Pasiphae's child by this mating, the Minotaur, was imprisoned within a maze (labyrinth) designed by Daedalus at the request of Pasiphae's husband, Minos.* After Daedalus helped the lovesick Ariadne* save Theseus* from death in the labyrinth—he gave her a ball of thread that enabled Theseus to retrace his steps—Minos imprisoned him (in, according to some accounts, his own artistic marvel, the labyrinth). Daedalus escaped with his son, Icarus, by creating wings of feathers and wax, but Icarus fell to earth and died because he flew too close to the sun, which melted the wax of his wings.

Danaans   The people of Danaus* (king of Argos*); the Greeks.

Danaids   The fifty daughters of Danaus,* king of Argos,* who, with one exception, killed their husbands, the sons of Aegyptus, king of Egypt.

Danaus   King of Argos.*

Dardanus   Ancestor of the people of Troy;* son of Teucer* or of Jupiter.* In some traditions, Dardanus arrived in Troy from Italy.

Deucalion   The Greek Noah; one of two survivors of the Great Flood sent by Jupiter* to punish sinful mortals. See Pyrrha.

Diana   Sister of Phoebus,* also called Phoebe;* goddess of the moon and of magic; often indistinguishable from Hecate.*

Dictynna   A Cretan goddess, identified with Diana.*

Diomedes (1) A companion of Ulysses.★ In a famous night expedition at Troy,★ the two killed a Trojan spy, Dolon, and a newly arrived Trojan ally, Rhesus,★ and his men. They then made off with Rhesus' wonderful horses. (2) A mythical king of Thrace★ who fed human flesh to his horses until Hercules★ took the horses away from him.

Dis God of (buried) wealth; god of the dead = Pluto.★

dryads Female tree spirits (nymphs) often pursued by (or in pursuit of) the god Pan.★

Eetion Father of Andromache;★ killed, along with his seven sons, by Achilles.★

Eleusis A city in Attica,★ famous as the site of the rites of the goddess Ceres★ (Greek Demeter).

Elysium The (underworld) home of the blessed dead.

Endymion A handsome youth with whom the Moon (Diana)★ fell in love, and who, in many versions of the myth, sleeps eternally.

Enispe A small town in Arcadia★ (Greece).

Epidauros A coastal town not far from Argos★ (Greece), famous for its temple of Aesculapius, the god of healing and medicine.

Erebus The darkness of death and the underworld; the underworld itself.

Erinys The goddess of vendettas, who avenges bloodguilt; often named either Megaera★ or Tisiphone.

Eryx Son of Venus★ and Hercules,★ in whose honor a mountain in Sicily (famous for its temple of Venus) was named.

Europa Daughter of Agenor, a king of Phoenicia (ancient Lebanon); sister of Cadmus, founder of Thebes★ (Greece); abducted by Jupiter★ disguised as a bull; mother of Minos,★ king of Crete.

Fate That which is spoken or decreed; destiny, fate.

Fescennine A ribald, farcical Italian song, sung at Roman weddings; one of the specifically Italian elements in Seneca's representation of Jason's★ wedding. See Camena.

Fortune An Italian goddess, (temperamental) bringer of produce and good luck.

Furies Vengeful spirits of the dead. See Erinys.

Gaetulians People of North Africa (Tunis and Morocco).

Garamantians People of Saharan Africa.

Getae Nomadic and barbaric Thracian (Balkan) people.

Gonoessa A small town near Sicyon, in the Peloponnesus (Greece).

Gradivus The stepping, marching god: Mars.★

Greater Bear See Arctus.

Gyrton Town in Thessaly★ (Greece).

Haemus A great Balkan mountain range.

Harpies Monstrous creatures, part bird, part woman, chased from their home by the twin sons of Boreas.★ See Calais;★ Zetes.

Hebrus   A Thracian river (modern Maritza) which flows into the Aegean.

Hecate   Goddess of moon, magic, and witchcraft, also of crossroads; often called Trivia, "three-way path." See Diana.

Hector   Chief Trojan warrior in the war at Troy;★ son of Priam;★ husband of Andromache;★ killed by Achilles.★ Hector's body was ransomed from the Greeks by Priam.

Hecuba   Wife of Priam;★ mother of Hector,★ Cassandra,★ Polyxena,★ Paris,★ and Helenus.★

Helen   Daughter of Jupiter★ (or Tyndareus)★ and Leda; wife of Menelaus,★ king of Sparta;★ awarded by Venus★ as a prize to Paris★ (son of Priam,★ who took her away to Troy★ (see Ida). Her abduction triggered the Trojan War. After Paris' death she was married to his brother Deiphobus.

Helenus   Twin brother of Cassandra★ and, like her, a prophet; one of the few male survivors of Trojan royal blood; subsequently became king of Buthrotum, in Epirus.

Helle   Daughter of Athamas and Nephele. Her mother saved her from being sacrificed and sent her and her brother Phrixus★ out to sea on the back of a sheep with a fleece of gold. Helle drowned in the Hellespont (named for her), but Phrixus traveled on to Colchis,★ where the sheep was sacrificed and became the Golden Fleece, the object of Jason's★ and the Argonauts' quest.

Hercules   Son of Jupiter★ and Alcmena.★ He sailed on the *Argo*★ but was left behind when his friend Hylas★ failed to return to the ship and Hercules stayed ashore too long searching for him. He was the strongest of Greek heroes; his bow, inherited by Philoctetes, was supposedly the critical weapon in the final struggle for Troy.★ Among his other labors, he killed the many-headed water snake, the Hydra,★ whose poison Medea★ wanted. His prowess at killing snakes first manifested itself when, as a child still in his cradle, he strangled two snakes that Juno★ had sent to kill him. Yet this masculine hero dressed as a maid when in love with Omphale.

Hercynian Forest   A vast forestland in ancient central Europe.

Hermione   Daughter of Helen★ and Menelaus;★ married to Pyrrhus,★ who was murdered by Orestes;★ finally married Orestes.

Hesperus   The evening star; the west.

Hippolytus   Son of Theseus★ and the Amazon★ Antiope.★

Hister   The river Danube.

Hyades   (1) Daughters of Atlas. (2) The Zodiacal constellation Hyades ("Rainers").

Hydaspes   A tributary of the Indus River.

Hydra   A many-headed snake killed by Hercules★ at Lerna.★

Hylas   See Hercules.

Hymen   (1) God of (marriage) feasts. (2) A song (hymn) sung at weddings.

Hymettus   The most southerly of the three major mountains in Attica,★ famous for its honey.

Hyrcanians   People who lived near the Caspian Sea.

Ida   A well-timbered mountain near Troy;★ the site of the beauty contest among the goddesses Pallas★ (Minerva), Venus,★ and Juno★ at which Paris★ awarded the prize to Venus★ because she promised to give him Helen★ as his wife.

Idmon   A prophet, one of the Argonauts.

Ilisos   A river in Attica.★

Ilium   Another name for Troy,★ derived from Ilus, the son of Tros (for whom Troy was named).

Iolcos   A city of Thessaly★ (Greece), modern Volos; home of Jason;★ port of departure for the *Argo*.★

Ionian   Asiatic or Athenian Greek, as opposed to mainland and particularly Peloponnesian (Mycenaean) Greek.

Isthmos   See Corinth.

Ithaca   An island in the Ionian Sea; home of Ulysses.★

Ixion   A mythical criminal who attempted to rape Juno★ but was tricked into making love to a phantom made of clouds instead. The offspring of this union were the centaurs. Ixion's son, Pirithous,★ attempted to rape Proserpina,★ wife of Dis★ and goddess of the dead.

Jason   Son of Aeson;★ husband of Medea;★ commander of the *Argo*.★

Juno   Wife and sister of Jupiter;★ patron of Argos★ and of Jason.★

Jupiter   Most powerful of the gods; lord of the thunderbolt; ancestor of the Cretan house of Minos.★

Laertes   Father of Ulysses.★

Laomedon   Father of Priam;★ cheated Neptune★ and Phoebus★ of their wages for building Troy;★ also cheated Hercules★ of his promised reward for saving Laomedon's daughter; as a consequence, Hercules attacked and captured Troy.

Lerna   (1) Home of the Hydra.★ (2) Fountain near Corinth.★

Lesbos   An Aegean island plundered by Achilles★ before the Trojan War.

Lesser Bear   See Arctus.

Lethe   The river of forgetting; one of the rivers of the underworld.

Leucate   An island in the Ionian Sea.

Libra   The zodiacal sign Libra.

Libya   General term for North Africa.

Lucifer   The "Bringer of Light," the morning star.

Lucina   The "Bringer to Light," goddess of childbirth.

Lycaon   "Wolfman." Arcadian king, father of Callisto★; changed into a wolf by Jupiter★ because he killed a human being as a sacrificial offering.

Lynceus   An Argonaut famous for his ability to see great distances.

Lyrnesos   A town in the vicinity of Troy.★

maenad   A woman "possessed" or maddened by the power of a god (usually Bacchus)★ and endowed with superhuman strength and subhuman ferocity.

Maeotis   The Sea of Azov and its environs.

Malea   A headland in the southern Peloponnesus (Greece).

Marathon   A coastal area of eastern Attica;★ home of a fierce bull killed by Theseus.★

Mars   God of war; lover of Venus.★ See Gradivus.

Meander   The Meander (now the Menderes) River, in Asia Minor (Turkey).

Medea   Daughter of Aeetes,★ king of Colchis;★ wife of Jason;★ stepmother of Theseus.★

Medes   Inhabitants of Parthia★ (ancient Iran).

Medusa   A deadly female monster whose hideous face turned anyone who saw her into stone; killed by the hero Perseus.

Megaera   See Erinys.

Meleager   See Althea.

Memnon   Son of Aurora (Dawn), the last ally to come to Troy's★ aid; killed by Achilles★ before the eyes of his mother and his uncle (Priam).★

Menelaus   King of Sparta;★ son of Atreus;★ brother of Agamemnon;★ husband of Helen.★

Minos   King of Crete; father of Phaedra★ and Ariadne.★

Minyae   (1) The people of the Minyius River, in Greece. (2) The Argonauts.

Molossians   People of Epirus famous for their dogs, "Dalmatians."

Mopsopia   Athens.

Mopsus   A prophet; one of the Argonauts.

Mothone   A town at the foot of Mount Pelion,★ in Thessaly★ (Greece); ruled by Philoctetes, whose bow (inherited from Hercules)★ the Greeks needed to procure the fall of Troy.★

Mycenae   A town near Argos;★ home of Agamemnon.★

Mysia   See Telephus.

naiads   Female water spirits (nymphs).

Nauplius   An Argonaut; later lured a Greek fleet to shipwreck because of his anger at the Greeks for their mistreatment of his son Palamedes.

Neptune   God of the (Aegean) sea, of horses, and of earthquakes; father of Theseus★ (Aegeus,★ who is Theseus' father in some versions, is himself essentially "the Aegean"); one of the gods who built Troy.★

Nereids   Female sea deities (nymphs); daughters of Nereus.★

Nereus   A lesser sea god; father of the Nereids★ and of Thetis,★ thus grandfather of Achilles.★

Neritos   An island near Ithaca★ in the Ionian★ Sea.

Nessus   A centaur (see Ixion) who attempted to rape Deianira, a wife of Hercules.★ Hercules killed him with a poisoned arrow, but to gain revenge before he died Nessus gave Deianira some of his poisoned blood, which he said would help her restore Hercules' love if he was ever unfaithful to her. Hercules was unfaithful, and he was given a cloak, tainted with Nessus' blood which caused him to die in agony.

Nestor   The oldest Greek warrior in the Trojan War. His home was Pylos,★ in the western Peloponnesus (Greece).

Niobe   A Theban princess who angered Phoebus★ and Diana★ by boasting that her children were more beautiful than they. As punishment, the two deities shot down all fourteen of Niobe's children with arrows, and she wept until she was turned to stone.

Notos   The southwest wind.

Nysa   A mountain, supposedly in India, associated with Bacchus.★

Oceanus   (1) A mythical river that flows round the world. (2) The Atlantic Ocean.

Oeta   A mountain in Thessaly★ (Greece), where Hercules★ died.

Oileus   An Argonaut; father of one of the two warriors named Ajax★ who fought at Troy.★

Olenus   A Greek town near modern Patras.

Ophiuchus   A constellation, now divided into two: the Snake Holder and the Snake.

Orestes   Son of Agamemnon.★

Orpheus   A Thracian singer, son of the Muse Camena,★ whose songs could beguile even trees and stones to move; an Argonaut. He was killed by maenads★ in Thrace:★ his head was torn off and it floated down the river Hebrus★ into the Aegean and across to Lesbos.★

Pallas   A goddess identified with Minerva (Athena); builder of the *Argo*.★ Pallas' citadel = the acropolis of Athens.

Pan(s)   Goat god(s), pursuers of (and pursued by) dryads.★

Pangaeus Mountain   A mountain in Thrace,★ near Philippi.

Paris   Son of Priam★ and Hecuba;★ abductor of Helen.★ See Ida.

Parnes   A mountain range in Attica.★

Parnethus   An area between Attica★ and Boeotia.

Paros   An Aegean island famous for its marble.

Parthia(ns)   An Iranian people, who became dominant in Persia about 250 B.C.

Pasiphae   Daughter of Sol★ (the Sun); wife of Minos;★ lover of a bull by whom she became mother of the Minotaur (see Daedalus); also mother of Phaedra,★ Ariadne,★ and Androgeos.

Patroclus   A close companion of Achilles★ at Troy.★ When Achilles would not fight because of his quarrel with Agamemnon,★ Patroclus was permitted to put on Achilles' armor and fight in his place. He was thus the "false Achilles." Hector★ killed him.

Pegasus   (1) A horse with wings, born from the blood of the dying gorgon Medusa.★ (2) The constellation Pegasus.

Pelasgians   Aboriginal, non-Greek-speaking inhabitants of Greece.

Peleus   Son of Aeacus,★ often associated with Mount Pelion,★ in Thessaly★ (Greece). Peleus killed his brother Phocus, then traveled to Phthia,★ where he was cleansed of bloodguilt but accidentally killed his purifier. In exile at Iolcus,★ he was again purified (by Acastus,★ son of Pelias).★ He was rewarded for his courage by being given Thetis★ as his bride. She bore him Achilles.★

Pelias   Uncle of Jason★ who usurped power at Iolcus★ and sent Jason on his quest for the Golden Fleece; killed unintentionally by his daughters, who dismembered and cooked him in the mistaken belief that they could rejuvenate him with Medea's★ spells and potions.

Pelion   A mountain in Thessaly★ (Greece).

Pelops   Son of Tantalus;★ father of Atreus;★ grandfather of Agamemnon★ and Menelaus;★ killed and dismembered by his father to provide a banquet for Jupiter★ but later restored to life. The Peloponnesus ("Island of Pelops") was thought to be named for him. Thus "Pelopian" often means "Peloponnesian" or "Corinthian," as Corinth★ guards the entrance to the Peloponnesus.

Pelorus   The northeast coast of Sicily, associated with Scylla.★

Penthesilea   Queen of the Amazons★ who led an army against the Greeks at Troy★ and was killed by Achilles.★

Peparethos   A small island off the coast of Thessaly★ (Greece).

Pergamum   The citadel of Troy.★

Periclymenus   Son of Neptune★ who could change shape; an Argonaut; killed by Hercules★ while he was in the form of a fly.

Perseis   Wife of Sol★ (the Sun); mother of Aeetes,★ king of Colchis;★ grandmother of Medea.★

Phaedra   Daughter of Minos★ and Pasiphae.★

Phaethon   Son of Sol★ (the Sun). Having persuaded his father to let him drive the solar chariot for a day, Phaethon lost control of the horses, caused great damage in heaven and on earth, and was finally struck by a thunderbolt from Jupiter.★ His body fell into the mythical river Eridanus. His sisters, who came there to mourn him were metamorphosed into trees, and their tears became amber.

Pharis   A small town near Sparta★ (Greece).

Phasis   The river Rioni★ (now in the Soviet Union), on which Medea's★ city, Colchis,★ was situated.

Pherae   A city in Thessaly★ (Greece); home of Admetus★ and Alcestis.★

Philoctetes   See Mothone.

Phlegethon   A fiery river of the underworld.

Phlyeis   A region of Attica.★

Phoebe   Goddess of the moon; sister of Phoebus.★ See Diana.

Phoebus   A god famous for his beauty, his bow and arrows, and his love of music; identified with the daylight and Sol★ (the Sun) and also called Apollo; one of the gods who built Troy.★

Phrixus Traveled on the golden-fleeced sheep with his sister Helle.★ Unlike Helle, he arrived safely in Colchis,★ his destination. See Helle.

Phrygia The area of Asia Minor (Turkey) in which Troy★ was situated.

Phthia A city in Thessaly★ (Greece) known for the ferocity of its inhabitants, notably Achilles.★

pietas Dedication to one's gods, country, and family.

Pindus A high mountain on the borders of Thessaly★ (Greece) and Epirus.

Pirene A Corinthian fountain from which Tantalus★ drank.

Pirithous Son of Ixion★ and friend of Theseus.★ He and Theseus went together into the underworld to carry off Proserpina,★ the wife of Dis.★

Pisa A town in the Peloponnesus (Greece); = Olympia.

Pittheus King of Troezen,★ in the Peloponnesus; father of Aethra, Theseus'★ mother.

Pleiades (1) A cluster of stars in the constellation Taurus.★ (2) Daughters of Atlas, the mythical giant who holds up the skies.

Pleuron A coastal town in Aetolia (Greece).

Pluto See Dis.

Pollux See Castor.

Polyxena Daughter of Priam★ and Hecuba;★ sacrificed on the tomb of Achilles,★ near Troy,★ at the end of the Trojan War.

Pompey A Roman politican and general of the first century B.C. who symbolized for many Romans the last days of freedom before the domination of the Caesars. He was defeated by Julius Caesar at Pharsalia, in Greece, in 48 B.C. and murdered in Egypt by a soldier named Achillas later in the same year. His body was left headless upon the seashore. Vergil in *Aeneid* 2.557 seems to be alluding to Pompey's death in his description of Priam's★ death, and Seneca seems to be echoing Vergil.

Pontus The Black Sea area, including the Roman province of Pontus.

Priam The last king of Troy★ and husband of Hecuba;★ he was twice left at the mercy of the Greeks when Troy was captured: first by Hercules,★ then by Agamemnon.★ Hercules spared his life; Pyrrhus,★ son of Achilles,★ murdered him on an altar. See Pompey.

Procrustes A highwayman who lived near Eleusis;★ he mutilated and killed travelers by putting them on a short bed and lopping off their extremities if they were tall, or by putting them on a long bed and stretching them if they were small; killed by Theseus.★

Prometheus A Titan★ who brought Jupiter's★ fire to mortals. For this offense he was chained to a crag on the Caucasus★ Mountain, where an eagle came daily to eat his liver. Each night the liver regrew; each day the eagle returned until Hercules★ killed it.

Proserpina Daughter of Ceres,★ goddess of crops; abducted by Dis★ to be his wife among the dead. Pirithous★ attempted to carry her off from the underworld with Theseus'★ help.

Proteus   The Old Man of the Sea, a divine or semidivine being who could change into many shapes and was also a prophet. He lived off the coast of Egypt near the site of the famous lighthouse of Pharos, near Alexandria.

Prothoüs   A Greek leader in the Trojan War who came from the region of Mount Pelion,★ in Thessaly★ (Greece).

Pylos   See Nestor.

Pyrrha   "The Fiery One"; wife of Deucalion.★ After the Great Flood, she and Deucalion regenerated the human race by throwing stones over their shoulders: those thrown by Deucalion became men, those thrown by Pyrrha became women.

Pyrrhus   Son of Achilles★ and Deidamia (whom Achilles raped on the island of Scyros;)★ killer of Priam★ and symbol of Greek brutality during the destruction of Troy.★

Python   A snake which inhabited Mount Parnassus, in Greece, and which was killed by Phoebus★ (Apollo) before he set up his oracle at Delphi.

Rhesus   See Diomedes (1).

Rhipaean Mountains   A more or less mythical mountain range in central Europe beyond which the people especially loved by Phoebus,★ the Hyperboreans (those who live beyond Boreas,★ the north wind), supposedly lived in a kind of earthly paradise.

Rhoeteum   A headland jutting into the sea not far from Troy,★ and the town on that headland.

Rioni   The modern name of the river Phasis★ (in the USSR), on which Colchis,★ home of Medea,★ was situated.

Salamis   An island off the coast of Attica,★ in the Saronic Gulf.

Sarmatians   Nomadic Slavic people living in parts of what is now the western Soviet Union and part of Eastern Europe, between the Vistula and the Don; culturally related to the Scythians.★

Scarphe   A small town in central Greece.

Sciron's Rocks   Precipitous cliffs between Athens and Megara; named for the bandit Sciron, who kicked passers-by into the sea from them. Sciron was killed by Theseus.★

Scylla   A voracious female seamonster with many doglike heads who lay in wait for sailors. Her traditional site in the works of later Greek and Roman writers is off the Sicilian coast. See Pelorus.

Scyros   An island off the coast of Euboea (Greece), where Thetis★ hid Achilles★ from Greek recruiters who wanted him to fight at Troy.★ See Achilles.

Scythians   Nomadic people of eastern Europe and Asia whom the Romans knew mostly from contacts in the areas adjoining the Black Sea; rendered as "Cossacks" in the translation. See Sarmatians.

Seres   The Chinese.

Sidonian   (1) Of Sidon in Phoenicia (modern Lebanon), or of a city colonized
by the Phoenicians, such as Carthage (in Tunis) or Thebes★ (in
Greece). (2) Colored with the crimson murex dye for which the
Phoenicians were famous.

Sigeum   A town near Rhoeteum★ and Troy,★ in Asia Minor (Turkey).

Sinis   A bandit who lived on the Isthmus of Corinth.★ He tied passing
travelers between two bent pine trees, which he then released; when
the trees sprang apart, the victim was torn in half. He was killed
by Theseus.★

Sinon   A Greek spy who persuaded the Trojans to take the Wooden Horse
into Troy.

Sirens   Mermaid-like singers whose beautiful voices lured sailors to destruction. Enchanted by the Sirens' song and eager to find its source,
sailors were drawn off course to a shore where they crashed on
treacherous rocks.

Sisyphus   Son of Aeolus★; king of Corinth★, famous for his ability to tell
lies; condemned after death to roll a stone up a mountainside forever
in retribution for his crimes.

Sol   The (god of the) Sun. See Phoebus.

Sparta   A city in the Peloponnesus.

Stymphalian birds   Mythical birds whose feathers were lethal shafts; killed
by Hercules.★

Styx   (1) An allegedly poisonous river in the Peloponnesus. (2) The most
famous of the rivers of the dead in Greco-Roman myth. An oath
sworn by the Styx was binding even on the gods.

Suebians   A Germanic tribe living east of the Elbe and known for its practice
of human sacrifice.

Sunion   A promontory on the coast of Attica.★ It was here, in some versions
of the myth, that Aegeus★ kept watch for the return of his son
Theseus★ from Crete and the Minotaur. When Aegeus saw the
black sails of the returning ship (Theseus had forgotten to change
them), he assumed his son was dead and threw himself into the
sea, thereafter known as the Aegean. A famous temple of Neptune★
(Poseidon) was later built on the promontory.

Symplegades   Mythical rocks in the sea which stood apart and separate until
a moving object tried to pass between them, at which time they
clashed together. The *Argo*★ had to sail through them. After its safe
passage, the rocks remained apart and never clashed together again.

Syrtes   Traditionally treacherous shallows off the coast of Tunis, in the Gulf
of Sidra.

Taenarum   A cave in the southern Peloponnesus through which Hercules★
dragged Cerberus★ out of the underworld; one of the traditional
entrances/exits of the underworld. See Avernus.

Talthybius   A Greek messenger. In the manuscripts he is the messenger

only for the appearance of Achilles'★ ghost in *Trojan Women*, but
it makes sense to give him the lines simply marked *nuntius*, "messenger," too.

Tanais   The Don River.

Tantalus   A king of Lydia (in Asia Minor [Turkey]); the son of Jupiter;★ a
wealthy and criminal ruler who sacrificed and cooked his own son,
Pelops,★ as a banquet for the gods. For his sins Tantalus was punished in one of two ways, according to various authors: (1) He was
imprisoned in the underworld, where he was forced to stand in
flowing water up to his neck, with grape clusters hanging above
his head. Whenever he reached up to eat or down to drink, the
grapes and the water receded beyond his reach. (2) He was left in
constant fear of a stone poised over his head, forever about to fall.
His daughter was Niobe.★

Tartarus   The deepest pit of the underworld, where the most terrible crim-
inals are punished; it was guarded by the dog Cerberus.★

Taurus   A mountain range running inland from Lycia, in southwest Turkey.
In Latin the name is suggestive of *taurus*, "bull," and the zodiacal
sign Taurus.

Taygetus   A mountain range near Sparta.★

Telemachus   Son of Ulysses.★

Telephus   Son of Hercules★ and Auge, the daughter of a king of Arcadia★
(Greece); he eventually became king of Mysia,★ in Asia Minor
(Turkey). His city was attacked by Achilles★ and the Greeks, who
mistook it for Troy,★ and Telephus was wounded by Achilles. The
only (and paradoxical) cure for the wound proved to be the rust
from the spear that had wounded him. (Thus Pyrrhus★ can claim
that Achilles' weapons cure as well as kill.)

Tempe   A valley in Thessaly★ (Greece).

Tenedos   An island off the coast of Troy,★ plundered by Achilles.★

Tethys   Wife of Oceanus;★ mother of Thetis,★ and thus grandmother of
Achilles.★ If Ceres★ is a kind of Mother Earth, Tethys is a kind of
Mother Ocean.

Teucer   Father of Dardanus★ and ultimate ancestor of the Trojan royal
house.

Thebes   (1) A city of Boeotia (Greece), founded by a Phoenician explorer
and exile, Cadmus; home of the prophet and Argonaut Mopsus.★
(2) A city in Asia Minor, home of Andromache.★

Thermodon   A river near the Black Sea, best known for its associations
with the Amazons.★

Theseus   Son of Neptune★ or Aegeus;★ stepson of Medea;★ famous as a
killer of monsters in and around Attica★ (see Marathon; Procrustes;
Sciron's Rocks; Sinis). Later he went to Crete, where he killed the
Minotaur. He left Crete with Ariadne,★ daughter of Minos,★ but

abandoned her on the island of Naxos. On his return to Athens he neglected to change the black sails on his ship, and Aegeus,★ interpreting them as a sign of his son's death, committed suicide (see Sunion). Theseus fought and defeated the Amazons★ and married their queen, Antiope,★ by whom he had a son, Hippolytus.★ He later married Ariadne's sister, Phaedra.★ Theseus is often treated by ancient writers as a semihistorical figure (as in Plutarch's *Lives*, where, as founder of the Athenian state, he is paired with the legendary founder of Rome, Romulus).

Thessaly   A region of north-central Greece, in which Jason's★ hometown of Iolcos★ is situated. Thessaly is also famous as the home of Achilles,★ who was born and raised there by the centaur Chiron.★ It is no less famous for its horses (and centaurs), and for its magic and witches. For many Roman writers, Thessaly is also ominous as the site of the battle of Pharsalia (48 B.C.), where Julius Caesar defeated the republican armies under Pompey.★

Thetis   Mother of Achilles★ and wife of Peleus.★

Thrace   A mountainous and barbaric area in what is now the border regions of Greece, Bulgaria, and Turkey. Its northern boundary was the river Danube, and it was bisected by the river Haemus.★ In Seneca's day only the part south of the Haemus was, strictly speaking, Thrace. The northern area was the province of Moesia. Thrace was the home of Orpheus.★

Thria   A lowland community in western Attica,★ near Eleusis.★

Thule   Probably Iceland.

Thyestes   See Atreus.

Tigris   A river running through present-day Turkey and Iraq; for all practical purposes, the easternmost limit of Roman influence in Seneca's day.

Tiphys   The helmsman of the *Argo*.★

Titan   (1) Sol★ (the Sun). (2) One of a family of giants who ruled the earth until their defeat by Jupiter★ and the Olympians, who imprisoned them under Mount Aetna.★

Titaressos   A river in Thessaly★ (Greece) which flows into the river Peneus. Seneca seems to think it flows into the Aegean.

Tityos   A son of Earth who attempted to rape Leto, the mother of Phoebus★ (Apollo) and Diana.★ He was punished in the underworld by having his ever-regenerating liver eaten by two vultures.

Tonans   The Thunderer (Jupiter).★

Trachis   A town in central Greece under the control of Achilles'★ family.

Tricce   A town in Thessaly★ (Greece).

Triptolemus   A hero of Eleusis,★ linked with the cult of Ceres★ and Proserpina.★

Tritons   Minor (and musical) sea divinites.

Troezen   A town on the east coast of the Peloponnesus.

Troy   A city on the Hellespont, twice conquered by the Greeks: first under Hercules,★ who was angered by the bad faith of its king, Laomedon,★ and then, in the next generation (when Laomedon's son Priam★ was king), by Agamemnon★ and a coalition of Greek leaders. The conquest was precipitated by the abduction of the Greek queen Helen,★ wife of Agamemnon's brother Menelaus,★ by Paris,★ son of Priam. Roman writers felt a special sympathy for the Trojans in their wars with the Greeks because of the tradition that Troy's founders originally came from Italy and that the Romans could trace their own ethnic origins to a refugee (Aeneas) who escaped from the second and catastrophic defeat of Troy by the Greeks (see Venus). It was rumored in the last half of the first century B.C. that Rome's Caesars intended to transfer the capital of the empire to a rebuilt Troy.

Tyndareus   King of Sparta;★ in some versions, father of Helen★ and her sister Clytemnestra, and of Castor★ and Pollux.★ Helen is often referred to as "daughter of Tyndareus."

Typhoeus   A monstrous, hundred-headed son of Earth who fought against Jupiter★ for control of the heavens; defeated and buried under Mount Aetna.★

Tyre   A city of Phoenicia (Lebanon), famous for its high living and its crimson dyes. See Sidonian.

Ulysses   Son of Laertes;★ the Roman Odysseus, generally treated unfavorably in Latin poetry because of his treacherous behavior, but presented as an exemplar of the suffering hero, worthy of comparison with Cato and Socrates, in Roman prose. The contrast is particularly sharp in Seneca: the Ulysses of *Trojan Women* is one of ancient tragedy's most villainous characters, but the Ulysses of Seneca's prose works is the embodiment of Stoic virtue.

Venus   Beautiful but faithless goddess of love; wife of Vulcan★ and lover of Mars;★ mother of Amor★ (Cupid)★ and, in Roman tradition, divine forebear of the Caesars because of their mythical descent from Aeneas, Venus' son by Anchises, a Trojan prince. In Latin the word *venus* often means essentially sexuality, even the sexual act.

Vulcan   The smelter of metals (Mulciber, in Latin); god of metalworking and fire, associated with volcanoes, especially Mount Aetna;★ husband of Venus.★

Xanthus   The main river in the vicinity of Troy.★

Zacynthos   An Ionian★ island near Cephallenia★ and Ithaca.★

Zephyr   The west wind; wind of springtime.

Zetes   See Boreas; Calais.